The How To Book Of
TEEN SELF DISCOVERY

The How To Book Of

TEEN.

Self Discovery

HELPING TEENS FIND
BALANCE, SECURITY & ESTEEM

Published in the United States of America by:
Planetary Publications
P.O. Box 66
Boulder Creek, CA 95006
(408) 338-2161

Manufactured in the United States of America by Baker-Johnson
Cover Design by Sandy Royall

Library of Congress Cataloging In Publication Data

Childre, Lew, Doc
    The how to book of teen self discovery : helping teens find balance, security & esteem / by Doc Lew Childre.
        p.   cm.
    ISBN 1-879052-18-0
    1. Adolescence - - Juvenile literature. 2. Teenagers - - Conduct of life - - Juvenile literature. 3. Adolescent psychology - - Juvenile literature. 4. Self-esteem in adolescence -- Juvenile literature.
    I. Title.
HQ796 . C458235   1992
305 . 23 ' 5 - - dc20   92-24296
                                                                    CIP
                                                                    AC

10 9 8 7 6 5 4 3 2 1

Table of Contents

Dedication

This book is dedicated to all the teenagers who
want to feel understood,
who want to feel more secure about who they are,
who want better relationships
with parents and friends,
and who want to find more fulfillment and fun
in the adventure of life.

If you are a parent, teacher or teenager who has to
deal with curfews, school, being understood,
pressures and all the other challenges associated with
growing up, *TEEN Self Discovery* presents *a new way*
of smoothing out the lumps and bumps through
practicing these tools, leading to more fulfillment
and self-security.

Though this material is written for teenagers, it is also
designed to help adults gain a better understanding of
both teenagers and themselves. Self Discovery is
"heart smart," regardless of age, sex, race, color or
religion. Hopefully, a better understanding of the
"common sense of the heart" can add to the quality of
your life and your buddies' as well. Please enjoy.

Respectfully,

The Doc

Thank You

More than 20 people from the Institute of HeartMath were involved in the creation of this book, including two residential artists who did the cover design and cartoon illustrations, writers, proofreaders, computer graphics and typesetting specialists, and many people whose examples — from their teenage years — have been used throughout this book. Thanks to all of you!

— the publishers

A Note to Parents

This book helps teens go to their heart to find inner security and understanding. It can be used by teens whether or not they have family support. However, the process works best if parents or other adults practice with the teens. A cooperative effort between adults and teens to relate to each other from the heart is *the missing ingredient for deeper bonding* and for bridging communication gaps. The bonding between parents and teens is more important to their well-being than just providing shelter, food and external conveniences. It is a vital necessity that is often ignored.

Bonding is establishing communication at the heart level which results in mutual respect and a deeper understanding of each other. Living under the same roof together, *without being heart-connected and understood at the feeling level,* has a detrimental effect on teens' future integration into society.

Institutions, especially schools, have been forced into

a vacuum left by the disintegration of family values and family connectedness. President Bush and many others are saying, "We have got to find ways to strengthen the American family." But how? Connecting more deeply at the heart level with oneself and others is an important part of the answer. Many families today are united in namesake, but are missing the sensitivities and care that foster true family connectedness. Children who don't experience sustained emotional bonding find it harder to learn self-control or to really care for themselves or others. Their hearts shut down. As a result, they are unable to learn as well in school.

A *Los Angeles Times* report showed that teens have a harder time saying no to drugs when they lack family bonding. Many teens who take drugs say they don't *feel* loved. They feel detached and afraid. Other teens say they are escaping a sense of hopelessness about life. These aren't the only reasons teenagers use drugs and alcohol, but they are major factors that teens themselves are reporting. These problems can only be remedied or prevented by a mutual effort on the part of adults and teens to communicate and understand each other's perspectives at a deeper level. Bonding fosters the kind of self-confidence that teens need in order to make decisions that may be unpopular with peers at a time in their lives when the need to belong is intense. Many teens join gangs because of a certain level of bonding that gangs offer.

Divorce has also taken its toll on family bonding. Studies show that, nationwide, 60% of youngsters feel they are to blame in a divorce and feel rejected by at least one parent; 50% live in families where the divorced parents stay angry; and one third of all children never see one of their parents again after divorce. Teenagers often go to school or out into the world carrying emotional baggage from unresolved issues at home.

We can't afford to ignore the statistics on what is happening in today's society. Basic survival is tougher, requiring much more energy — both parents needing jobs, children being raised at day care, 24% of all children living with only one parent who has to work, keep house, and pay the bills. A recent *Los Angeles Times* poll revealed that parents feel frustrated and guilty because they lack time to supervise their children. 78% of parents polled gave themselves a C, D or F grade in teaching their children moral values. Another national survey found that *1 in 5 teenagers had not had a 10-minute conversation with a parent in the past month.* Overall, parents in today's world spend 10-12 *fewer* hours per week with their teenagers than parents did in the '60s. The irony is that those of us who were teenagers in the '60s realize how much less time we spent with our parents compared to previous generations.

So how can busy parents and adults bond with teens and inject more quality care into their already demanding schedules? Time may not always be the real issue. It's what parents and adults choose to do with the time they have. How much time do you spend feeling under stress or looking for ways to escape or release stress? *Self-Discovery* shows you how to manage your own mental and emotional energies to prevent stress and achieve time effectiveness. Most parents do care, but their care gets diluted by their own lack of mental and emotional self-management.

The biggest problem, according to teenagers, is that parents don't listen. Many parents feel that teens don't listen. Then, when teens don't act like they are expected to, parents throw up their hands and ask, "Where did I go wrong?" Becoming "Heart Smart" is an effective facilitator for overcoming this dilemma. Learning how to listen to each other from the heart with sincere attention is a first step. Most people just listen to each other from the head, with their own thoughts and emotions running through their minds at the same time. This causes gaps in communication, leading to judgments, resentments and distance between people. Read the "Deep Listening" chapter for a better understanding of how to listen from the heart and improve communication.

Self-Discovery creates a joint venture between your head and your heart so that you can manage your stress and be who you really are. The head and heart both have important roles to play in the efficient operation of the human system. When your head and your heart are out of sync, it leads to insecurity, inner turmoil and conflict with others. When they work together in balance, it leads to creative problem-solving, self-security and esteem. Life seems to re-arrange itself so you have more time for your real priorities, like family bonding and deeper communication. Then life becomes more rewarding and fulfilling. *Self-Discovery* increases in teens and adults as security is built from within.

Parents and teens can embark on *Self-Discovery* together as a fun adventure. By reading the different chapters and discussing the issues covered in the book together, they can share examples from their own lives on the everyday concerns that adults and teens both face. This can open the door for a lively discussion on stress-producing head reactions and the heart smarts' responses that reduce stress and help you be your true self. Take a look at the Ready Reference pages in Chapter 18 and see how they apply to your life. Start with the smaller situations, then the more serious problems get easier to deal with as you develop your *heart smarts*. The book is directed to teens and written in a fun style that most young people can relate to. But adults can quickly translate the examples to similar situations in their own lives and apply the same how-to's for their Self-Discovery. Family bonding is built and strengthened when adults and teens talk together about deep issues that speak to the heart.

Sincerely,

Doc Lew Childre

Self Discovery

1

Let's Meet

Your teenage years can be some of the most awesome and challenging times of your life!

People seem to always remember their teenage years as times when they felt daring, adventurous and spontaneous! And, they often remember those years as some of their more difficult times — with a lot of mixed emotions, and a lot of choices to make. As a teenager yourself, you may have experienced the feeling that you were misunderstood, especially by adults. Hey, it's true. Adults do have a hard time understanding teenagers. But maybe, sometimes, the misunderstood feeling is really just *you* trying to understand how to put the pieces of your life puzzle together. Sometimes, these feelings can feel really big, like your puzzle must have thousands of pieces to it. That can seem overwhelming, leaving you with stress.

The feelings of being misunderstood, confused,

with mixed-up emotions and stress are not isolated to just teens. These are feelings that parents, teachers — everyone — experiences from time to time. Often these feelings seem more intense or come more frequently for teenagers than they would for an adult or young child. If you were to stop a minute and realize all that is happening to the human system during the teenage years, you would have more understanding and compassion* for yourself. It's a process of change. The emotional and hormonal changes can make everything feel exaggerated and out of balance. That childhood feeling of fun and excitement for a new day gets colored by new emotions and feelings that might not be clear, making some days feel like a roller coaster ride on a rainy day. The hormonal changes can directly affect your emotional responses to people and situations.

Let's get real. There is a real gap between a lot of adults and teenagers. Teenagers often feel that they get the usual, standard, passed-down formulas for life from adults and they write adults off as not really understanding *them*. So, they ignore a lot of knowledge that adults have gotten through trial and error in life. When you are a teenager, coming into your own sense of yourself, becoming responsible for who you are, you feel right about your feelings and feel like you know what you know. But, adults also feel like they know what they know and are right about what they are trying to pass down, be-

* **compassion** — a deep caring that does not cross the line into sympathy

cause they gained that knowledge from trial and error experience. So, teenagers and adults are just not understanding each other.

Here's an example: a sixteen-year-old wants to go to a big party. Everyone is going to be there. Her parents know that a certain street gang is going to be there, too, and they try to tell their daughter. She doesn't believe it will be a problem or see the possible consequences, gets really angry that her parents won't let her go, and locks herself away in her room, depressed for hours. Her parents have a certain trial and error wisdom, but because the teenager doesn't feel understood in so many other areas, she can't *hear* or respect her parents in that one area.

I wish my parents could remember what it feels like to be a teenager — just one time!!

Teens need more sensitivity from adults due to the extra **amped-up*** emotions that teens have. Adults can remember some of what it was like being a teenager, but hey, they don't walk in a teen's shoes. Parents and teachers could help more if they let teens know that they can't always understand them. And, because they can't, it's sometimes hard for teenagers to respect the useful trial and error knowledge being passed down to them.

This may not be your exact situation, but I bet you can think of your own examples that fit your case. So, what can teenagers do? As I got security* in my own self, I discovered more and more that it's not that some adults *won't* understand, but that they simply *can't always* understand. Just knowing that can cut out a lot of hurt, pain, and depression that comes when you feel that you aren't understood. I discovered that, hey, my parents really did love me and that sometimes they just didn't know how to show me the love they really did have for me.

You as teens will come out all right by building your own *heart smarts* — your own security in your own hearts. In just doing this, you can help create an atmosphere for more possible understanding all around. After all, everyone changes, so parents and teachers would be experiencing change also, adjusting to your growth and changes. It might cause adult insecurities to rise,

* **amped up** — fiery emotional vitality, positive or negative

* **security** — a sense of peace, feeling good inside, the confidence of inner knowingness

too. Adults are working on bettering themselves just like teenagers are. The sooner there is a *bridge* in communication, the sooner everyone can have understanding. Hopefully this book can help lay some planks for that bridge, and the adults and teenagers can have fun crossing it together.

So, where do we start? *Heart smarts* is about being responsible for your actions and reactions so you can make your day-to-day life feel more like surfing — by *riding* the waves of emotion instead of letting the waves engulf you. That's how you can build that heart security and self-esteem* that's just right for you. Wouldn't it be great to combine the essence of being adventuresome and playful with the feelings of clarity and inner confidence? This book is filled with "how to" examples for your own *Self-Discovery*, giving you practical exercises that you can apply to life, *the excellent adventure*. Maybe there is a way to make it all better by taking a deeper look at ourselves. That's streetsense.*

You've all heard the expression from adults, "I wish I knew that when I was your age." And, most adults really *do* wish they had known what they know *now*, when they were teenagers. That knowledge would allow people to take a shortcut instead of a long, winding road to self-discovery. We're all learning and growing in life. It's not that any road, silky or bumpy, won't get us

* **self-esteem** — a confidence filled with vitality; a deep belief in yourself, even if others don't at times
* **streetsense** — common sense understanding; obvious make-sense

where we want to go, but sometimes a smooth ride can save energy and time. Learn to ride through life the smart way — use your *heart smarts*.

A Note from the Publishers:

This book was written by Doc Lew Childre, with fun facilitation from many people at the Institute of HeartMath, including teens. Our intentions are to share with you some of the shortcuts we've learned while using the system Doc created, called HeartMath. These shortcuts have helped us to release stress and gain the confidence that comes from getting to know yourself. If you haven't heard of the Institute of HeartMath, let us introduce ourselves to you. We are a group of friends, made up of musicians, artists, writers, inventors and educators, who love creating books and tapes designed to help individuals live more efficiently, which we feel means learning to live smart from the heart.

Like many other creative groups, we're just trying to make a contribution to help people have more peace and fun in their life's experience. As a group of friends, we are practicing efficiency* with our energies — mental, emotional and physical. Because of this, we eliminate much of the stress in our lives and have a lot of fun.

We're a very down-to-earth bunch of people who take care of business but know how to throw a good party, too. We sure enjoy the opportunity to share with you what has proven to bring more fun and enjoyment to our lives!

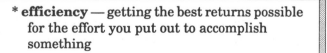
* **efficiency** — getting the best returns possible for the effort you put out to accomplish something

2

The Heart
A Smart Place to Start

It really is your choice — a life full of choices. Should I go out tonight or stay home and do extra studying? Okay, off the top...let's get real. It's your life and you're trying to do what you feel is right. Still, people everywhere — parents, friends and teachers — are all trying to tell you what you should do, or not do, or what you shouldn't have done, etc. Stressful, huh? So, where do you go when you want to have the power to do what you want to do, yet not feel stressed out by the choice you have made? Perhaps, you could go to your heart!

A lot of times when we come up against choices, our natural tendency is to weigh out our choices from the head. So, let's talk about the heart and the head and how the heart can help remove confusion and stress from choices.

Let's use a computer as an example of how the heart can work. If you saw your heart as a computer, it might have many programs to it, more than you might realize. Computers are what hold programs and data. So programs and data could be reactions and feelings to all types of situations. Positive data would be clear, positive feelings. Here are some examples:

•A good, secure feeling that comes when sitting under a favorite tree with the sun warming your face.

•The fun, excited feeling you get when you see your buddies again after being away on vacation.

•A soft, happy feeling when you're greeted by your puppy.

•The satisfaction of putting your all into studying for a test and seeing positive results for your efforts.

•The fun and excitement of seeing your favorite group in concert, or going to a party that felt like it was the best time you ever had.

There are many, many more programs to the heart computer. We all have them, and they're ours to discover.

Some people might say the head is like a computer, and I would agree. But, let's look at the heart as the central computer and the head as a subterminal that takes its commands from the central computer, which would be the heart.

The Heart

When people talk about the heart, a lot of times it is referred to in ways of sentiment, like a greeting card. Emotional reactions and sentimental feelings often start from a true heart feeling, but that feeling can get lost in over-worked emotions and thinking. A true heart feeling is clear, buoyant, and solid, like the examples I just gave. Here's an example from a friend of how the heart feeling can get lost in over-worked emotions, sentiment and thinking:

"When my parents split up, my heart felt like I wished I could help them feel happier because I loved them both so much. I felt a lot of true care for them. Those were the true heart feelings I had about them splitting up. Then, I started thinking, which triggered emotions and sentiment. I was afraid of the future and kept remembering the good times in the past that I thought would be lost forever. The more I thought, the more intense and larger my emotions got. Soon I was totally lost in a huge ocean of overwhelming emotions and completely confused. I let my emotions of fear, disappointment, and loss get so blown up that I couldn't even communicate my true care and original heart feelings. Instead, I would try to talk to my parents and would get frustrated and angry and it would end up in a mess of misunderstandings. After wearing myself out by letting so much of my energy pour out from over-blown emotions, I finally had nowhere else to go but back to the start, which was my heart.

"I started seeing that the most effective talks with my parents would happen when I kept my emotions balanced and in control. I had more clarity and could say what I *really* felt in my heart. Then, they could understand more easily what I really felt and wanted to say to them. My relationship with them became more of what I had wanted, as I practiced this every time I would talk to them."

Emotions are not bad. They add color to our lives.

But they can also create confusion and give you a real workout if you don't keep them in balance. Some people think of emotions and sentiment, like in the previous example, as the heart. I feel that emotions and sentiment come out of what is a true heart feeling. But, through a process of over-thinking and overreacting to the thoughts and emotions, the true feeling is lost. So, when I'm talking about the heart I'm giving a wider viewpoint than most people understand. I'm not talking about mushy, heavy, sentimental emotions. I'm talking about the true power of the heart — true caring — the smartest place to start! The heart computer would also have programs that enable us to make smooth calculations and data comparisons from a higher intelligence, the intuition*. Heart intuition is the smarter part of yourself. The heart is *way* smart — the seat of powerful wisdom. But, it would come user-friendly, so you could easily access programs of *streetsense*. Streetsense programs bring you common sense, along with power, clarity, balance and honesty — all the qualities of the ultimate you. And, they bring you a lot of fun, too!!!

The Head

Your head (brain/mind) is an important part of you. It's like an endless machine filled with lots of potential. People are always telling teens, "Use your head," meaning "Don't just react, think things through." School is

* **intuition** — to see into it, a knowledge or understanding that comes from inside yourself

mostly about learning all the ways we can use our heads for reading, writing, math, analyzing, thinking, memorizing and more. You'd have a hard time getting around in the world without a good head on your shoulders. I mean, really — without the head, how would you even know how to open a door, or drive a car?

Without the balanced wisdom of your heart, your head can also think itself right into misery. Your head thoughts can make you depressed, angry, conceited, hateful and trigger all sorts of emotions that don't feel good and often hurt others. *Getting heart smart is about building a joint venture between your head and your heart.* When you get these two parts of you working cooperatively together, then your thoughts and emotions work for you instead of against you.

If you let your head run the show all by itself, without the balance of getting data and comands from the central computer (the heart), you might experience what's known as a "crash." That's when you're so stressed out your system has stopped working efficiently and you usually have to go back to the heart and "restart." If you find yourself wondering, "Why does this keep happening? No one understands," it's usually a signal that your head is in a loop (going around in circles). When your head gets in a loop, it rationalizes and justifies trying to defend its point of view to compensate for a *lack* of satisfied feelings. Also, it can color your true feelings about things by using judgments, "poor-me's," unfulfillment, frustrations, etc., trying to make the self feel better about a situation or just feel happy with itself. But this doesn't usually work. Don't short-change your head. Go back to your heart feelings and intuition for more data and input. Select a new program. As you use your heart *with* your head, you can unlock your full potential and become your true self. That's *Self-Discovery*.

Here is an example a friend wrote to help you understand how the head and the heart are different, but can work together in balance:

"One particular week I was late getting to school every day. My first period teacher was seriously on my case. So, Friday morning I made sure I was ready to leave early so I could get there on time. I was on the freeway and came up on a traffic jam. Well, the way the traffic was moving, I knew it was going to be awhile before I even saw my exit. I started thinking from my head, 'I'll never make it on time! The one day I make an extra effort, and now this!' I felt like I wanted to blow

**I wish someone could understand me.
I guess I'd better understand myself!**

the horn, give everyone the finger and swear. I felt frustrated and impatient and I just knew my teacher wouldn't believe me. She'd think I made it up, for sure!

"All that was crashing around inside me. That's a lot of energy I was wasting on something I couldn't change in that moment. I was also making an assumption about the reaction of my teacher before the actual moment of explanation. About the only thing I could change was to go to my heart and realize, 'All right, I'm here and I have to wait for traffic to move on. When I get to school I'll explain what happened, the best I can, to my teacher.' Just remembering to go to my heart helped me feel calmer. In my heart, I knew that reacting wouldn't change the time of day or move the traffic. So, why feel uptight and start my day off with an edgy feeling? Besides, I remembered hearing that doctors and scientists have proven that when your emotions go into negative reactions, certain hormones are released which have a negative effect on your whole system. The negative reactive energy can build up over a period of time and cause disease of a physical nature. From just taking a moment to remember to go to my heart, I saw the situation in a new way. My heart said, 'Hey, maybe this traffic jam could be used for a little time to slow down and get calm. Then I could better handle the rest of my day, my teacher, and whatever else might pop up.'"

Okay, so you might say, "How obvious!" or, "I already knew all that!" *Exactly*. It's streetsense. It may not be new logic, but how often do you *really* use your own heart power to save yourself from stress? "Heart Power" means that you can store energy or power by choosing to use the heart, which operates more efficiently than the head does all by itself. An access code or password to get into the central computer could be as simple as "time out," taking a moment to pause and say, "Okay, heart...." (putting your concentration and energies into the area of your heart) — "Is what I'm about to do or say really going to be an efficient and smart choice, or a choice that will bring me undesired results later?" Taking that moment to access your heart computer is an example of being *heart smart.* Even though a yell or scream might have felt good in the moment of reacting, it would have left you feeling an inner stress mess to clean up later. Remember, earlier we talked about the term "crash," which is what can happen if you use just the *head* and decide not to follow the computer read-out from the *heart.* But, by using your head to follow a heart read-out instead, you could save a lot of energy and time, making your system more efficient and effective. It really does make life a lot more fun!

Let's go to another example: you want to go out Friday night. Your parents say yes, but they give you a curfew that doesn't seem fair. This isn't what you wanted them to say! Now, here come your choices — are you going to respond from the head or from the heart?

• *Stress out, freakout!* (Here we go again!)

You yell, you scream, you slam the door! "They just don't understand, they treat me like a kid!" Feeling stress?!! Suddenly, the fun idea of Friday night is feeling not so fun. Whether you physically react or just feel all the above reactions inside, don't kid yourself, it's still stress. You *can* change the program.

— *Freeze Frame* —

Before we go on to the second choice, let's "freeze frame" this example for a minute and talk in streetsense terms about how energy works. **Freeze-Frame** means stop and take a focused look. One of the laws of physics says that every action (inside or outside of yourself) has an equal or opposite reaction. In other words, it could mean, "what you put out, you get back." If you put out uncontrolled emotions, you get back an action or reaction equal to what you put out! Put out responsible emotional control (heart power), and you will get respect back. Your efforts in using heart power and emotional control could result in **you** feeling that you are being responsible. That feels good inside! You will see the payoff that comes from focused effort, just like you would with anything that is respected and appreciated.

The heart games we're talking about can show results *fast* if you truly play the games. In fact, even in the first effort your payoff will be visible, just in the sense of balance and reduced stress you will feel. You might even get a later curfew or not get one at all. Even if the curfew doesn't go your way, you still come out really good because you have saved yourself from processing all that stress. Stress can leave you in a lot worse shape than having to come home early would have. Certain disciplines are a part of growing up. If you face them maturely from the heart, the patterns change more quickly and in your favor. In addition, your efforts will be building higher self-esteem and heart power in *you!* It's just streetsense — **what you put out you get back!** Put out balanced responsibility and you get back flexibility.

Remember, we were talking about the curfew that didn't seem fair. Let's try out the heart example:

• Okay, so maybe it's not what you wanted them to say. Maybe you feel you are responsible enough to stay out later, and maybe that's true. But, let's just look at this from a streetsense standpoint. The first reaction (head response) spends a lot of energy. In turn, it cuts back your potential fun level for the rest of the night and leaves that uncomfortable feeling in the house. It's streetsense to realize you can't have maximum fun with stress and frustration crashing through your system. In this situation, a heart response might be, "Hey, all right, so I didn't get the curfew I wanted, but I've got five hours of fun ahead of me anyway!"

The *heart smart* way to react to situations that don't seem to be in your favor would be to go to your heart computer and select programs that can help you bail out (rescue) the situation. Try a"creative" program — look at having five hours as a game. How can you spend your time and divide it up to get the most out of it? A creative program helps you to see life situations like a game or puzzle, where day-to-day situations that seem like problems can be turned into adventures! These types of programs can feel like power packs and high jumps in the video game world.

Another helpful program you could use would be **appreciation** — seeing the wider picture. You could be too focused on the part of the situation that looks like a problem. Take a wider view of life and appreciate having a party to go to and being healthy enough to go. Appreciate parents that care enough to give you a curfew, even though it's *legal* to want to negotiate it after you've demonstrated maturity and responsibility. As you use *heart smarts* to change your own attitude, it magically can cause your parents to have the flexibility you would desire. Try it!

These heart computer programs are *powerful*. And, every time you choose to use the heart instead of just reacting from your head first, you build more and more power. The heart's power has a lot of magnetic energy. The more you use it, the more that magnetic energy attracts to you the opportunities and situations that your heart would truly desire. As my English friend, Robert, would say, "Let's have a smashing good time!"

In this last example, if you were to use the heart and choose balanced, responsible actions, you would build respect. In time, you could give your parents good reason to give you a later curfew, or maybe they would even let you be the one who decides when it's time to come home. However, really, the best payoff you would find in choosing to use your heart power would be minimum or no stress, and maximum fun time to have with your friends. That's making time and energy count, making it quality time! So, come on heart, let the good times roll!!!

Self
Discovery

3

Heart-FM
Your Inner Security Station

Security — what does that word mean in relation to you? You know, that feeling that you have in those moments when your world seems right? Sometimes life provides us with situations, parents, or relationships that help us feel secure, but sometimes it doesn't. If secure situations are taken away for whatever reason, we're left with our own hearts to pick up the pieces in some way and try to find security again. *Happiness is having that feeling of security within ourselves no matter what life brings us.*

Inner security, once you've got it, is something that nothing or no one can take away from you. Also, no one but yourself can give you that security. It's something you build yourself, sort of like building a secret fort in the woods or knitting a blanket that you can wrap yourself in when you're cold. So this chapter is really about you and your own inner security. That's what people seem to be wanting. Children look for security in their parents. Family bonding helps build that sense of security. Teenagers and adults look for security in relationships or school or jobs. Looking for inner security in yourself means developing a bond with your own heart. Security is built in the heart. So that means that heart smarts is about you and your own heart.

In the computer age people can come to finally understand that everything is made of frequencies of energy — including your thoughts, feelings, and emotions. You could compare it to listening to the radio. There are all kinds of radio stations: rock n' roll, heavy metal, blues, pop. You might listen to different ones, depending on what mood you're in at the time. You might listen to pop music on the way to a party because it would make you feel happy and upbeat. If you're feeling sad, you might feel like listening to blues. When you're feeling like rocking, you'll select rock music of your taste. Different kinds of music and different kinds of emotions are frequencies, just like your heart has its own *core frequencies* deep inside. Some of the innermost frequencies of your heart computer are: forgiveness, appreciation, kindness and love. They may sound like mushy feelings, but they are all power tools that make you feel good and release positive hormones into your system. Look at them as power frequencies that you can turn your dial to, when dealing with yourself and others in your day-to-day life. Being able to turn your own dial and access these deeper heart frequencies gives you the inner confidence of knowing you are in control, and that's when you find the peace of having true inner security.

So let's look at a few simple ways that you can access heart frequencies or heart intelligence programs and grab hold of that radio dial that you have access to inside your heart.

1. Don't look for it outside yourself.

It's really easy in life to look for security from parents, friends, teachers, and jobs. Let's say you are talking to your girl/boyfriend on the phone and when you hang up she/he doesn't say, "I love you, too" or whatever you might want her/him to say. So you feel uncared for, insecure, wondering if she/he does love you, and you feel unseen. Or, let's say your father has always wanted you to graduate from high school and go on to be a doctor or lawyer, but you want to be an artist. He gets angry after you sincerely tell him about it, then shuts off his heart and stops talking to you. It hurts and you feel insecure about his love and whether he'll support you after all. These are both situations where you looked for confirmation from someone you love and felt insecure when you didn't receive any approval. Instead of being resentful because someone didn't do what you thought or expected them to do, go within yourself and remember that life is about building your own inner security. Activate a core heart frequency. Make an effort even if you don't feel like it at the time. Activate love or forgiveness or appreciation for the good times that you have had together. Put that kind of frequency out instead of despair, anger or resentment, and see if you don't feel better. You never know how things can work out. It could get better. That's an example of a conscious heart choice that can bring a wider viewpoint or a creative solution that wasn't available to you before you activated your core heart frequency. The more you practice activating these frequencies of forgiveness, appreciation, kindness and love, the easier it becomes to switch to them when you need them. It's like using the pre-set buttons on your radio!

Often in life, you just don't get what you were hoping for. When you get disappointed about something it can drain you emotionally. So go back to your heart for a positive frequency for your next step. When something really drastic happens in life beyond your control, like your friend is killed in a car accident, you'd probably go deep in your heart because the heart gently comforts

By using your heart, you can dial up efficient programs in life. Then, you aren't the victim of other people's thoughts and programs. It makes sense!

the pain of loss. If the heart comforts and guides you in tragic situations, then it's streetsense that heart guidance in regular day-to-day situations would bring more fun, peace and efficiency in your life. That's Self-Discovery!

Here's an example from a friend's life. Maybe it will help explain:

"I was a model at 14 years old — not too long ago — and never thought I was very pretty, but other people did. Many people think that modeling is a wonderful and glamorous world but, in truth, there's a lot more to it. It's a hard business because it's based on how you look. That means that you are being judged on who you are on the outside and not who you really are on the inside. I would continually look to people to confirm that I was beautiful, and when they didn't, I'd feel insecure inside. Being judged by my appearance was hard to deal with, so I'd go to other areas to get confirmation of who I was inside, like my close friends and my mother and father. They helped, but still I finally had to go inside myself to find some peace and security. Another area where I looked for security was in relationships. When I would get into one, in my mind I would think, 'Who do they want me to be? What can I do for them so they'll love me?' I'd put everything I had into making the relationship work, and if it didn't, I'd feel empty.

"So I had these images of who I was, this model or this cute girlfriend, that gave me a plastic security but these weren't real. I always thought that people wanted something from me, like sex, for example, and in turn I'd cut my heart off. I'd enjoy the closeness and intimacy, but in truth, I would sometimes be doing it more for them than for me. I thought I could get approval or security through them loving me. I finally had to ask, 'Who am I inside myself? Maybe I need to look within myself for the answer and not keep trying to get others to give it to me. Maybe I'm not all these identities — maybe I'm someone else.'

"Starting to ask these questions was the first step on a fun adventure that I'm still on, discovering all the different parts of who I am and putting my own puzzle together. I've found that going inside for security has a much better return than looking for it in those around me. It takes practice, noticing day-to-day when I look to someone else for confirmation of who I am. So I just keep going back inside and I can see that everything that I need is within me. Knowing that truly makes me feel good."

So remember, don't go for security outside yourself. Now, back to the ways that heart frequencies really work to build inner security.

2. Don't judge yourself.

Everyone can fall victim to making judgements about themselves. It's hard not to. It's a common trait to criticize and judge yourself from the head. It almost feels like the natural thing to do. Everyone wants to improve themselves and become a better person. Judging or beating yourself will only drain you and make you feel bad inside. It instills a guilty feeling, convincing you that you're a bad person. I can remember when I wanted to try to communicate better in class, as well as with my friends and teachers. As I was speaking, I felt insecure and couldn't get my point across. I felt like I was a dummy and a misfit. I felt like I never would be able to talk at all. When I finally stopped judging myself and felt compassion for myself instead, I could just say, "Oops, there's that thing again where I can't express how I feel. Maybe if I slow down, get in my heart, forgive myself and feel compassion for myself, I can try to talk again." Guess what? It worked. I saw how the energy of judgment, and feeling that things are hopeless, dragged me down and kept me from being able to change. It just made life no fun. The heart program of forgiving myself, making things *no big deal*, allowed me to cut through feeling guilty for not being perfect and enabled me to move on. Then I could do something *positive* about the problem. So in the end, it is a lot more efficient to just love yourself, see the areas you want to grow in and just do the best you can do. It isn't worth it to judge yourself.

3. Give yourself pats on the back.

When you do things that are hard for you and accomplish something, appreciate yourself for it. You really are a good person, trying to do your best. Let's say there's a subject in school that's really hard for you, like science. It could be that it's really easy for your friend, Mary. Maybe it's her best subject. But, maybe she's not so good in music, which is your best subject. So you really can't compare. You can just do your best and make the effort, even if it's difficult for you. Then, just appreciate yourself for doing the best you can do. Appreciation is one of those core heart power frequencies that makes a difference in whether you have the energy to accomplish something and see it through, or not. Go for it! Appreciate the part of yourself that tries.

4. Do things for people.

One of the biggest energy boosters in life is caring for someone else. Not only does it feel good, it also puts capital into your *inner security account*. So when activating heart frequencies, you put investments into an inner heart account. Every time you choose to forgive yourself or another, or you make an effort to feel compassion, or to do something nice and caring for someone else, or express the love you feel in your heart, you are depositing heart energy into your *inner security bank*. Here's an example:

"My uncle, who worked at the coliseum, gave me tickets to a Billy Joel concert. My best friend, Mike, loved Billy Joel and he really liked this girl, Susan, at school. I knew these tickets would be the perfect lead-in for him to ask her out. So I had a choice. I could have gone to the concert myself with a friend, but I thought to myself, maybe it would be more fun to give Mike the tickets. Well, I did, and he was blown away! He took Susan to the concert, they had the time of their lives, and they're still going out today. It felt good to put someone else's interests before mine and treat someone like I would like to be treated. I gave Mike the tickets not because I wanted him to like me, but because I just truly wanted to give him a gift from my heart. Giving to someone, just because you can, makes you feel good inside."

That good feeling that you gain is that cash or income that we're talking about. When you invest in doing good things and running your life more efficiently through the heart, you can then draw on that energy from your positive bank account at those moments when you really need it. It's a lot like when you pick up your life supply in a video game and you draw on it while you're firing at whatever is coming at you. Instead of firing at problems with anger or frustration, which drains your account, you can fire at them from the inner part of your heart and get them with heart frequencies. The magical thing that you find out, through trial and error, is that heart frequencies and love get the job done faster. They are more efficient and can bring you a whole lot more quality and fun in return. If you've already reacted with anger or judgment and are caught up in that negative, frustrating energy, try switching your station. Tune up that radio dial in your heart, even though you might not feel like it right then. Just give it some extra effort. It still works. Conscious heart is a bailout and can be a lot of fun.

So try making efforts to build yourself a secure foundation within yourself. Once you have that bottom-line heart **connection**, whatever comes your way can be an add-on, but not something that takes your security away. You can only find out by trying it out and practicing it for yourself, like I did and **still have fun doing** every day. Practicing could be a joke compared to what you gain from doing it. People just don't think to practice it. The true security you could be looking for is within you, just waiting for you to **discover** it.

5. Don't let your situation in life discourage you.

You may be someone who doesn't have parents to relate your problems to. That can cause some disadvantages while growing up, and just trying to survive is tough in many cases. This makes finding the security in your own heart even more important. Even if you have parents, you still need to develop your own inner problem-solving ability. In maturing, you learn finally that you can't depend on other people for your peace and true security. Whether you have parents or not, accepting what is and going for growth finally gives you the strength to take care of yourself. Your heart is your best buddy, after all is said and done. Some of the best success stories in life come from people who have started out in broken homes and disadvantaged environments. If you practice using your heart smarts, you stand a good chance of making advantages out of disadvantages. Your heart can guide you more easily through the tough times in life as you learn to bond more with your deep heart.

6. Discover more friends you can bond with.

You can have surface level friendships, but really bonding with someone comes when there's a deeper heart connection. This allows you to feel understood and wanted. Some teens go all through school and never experience a real heart connection with more than one or two people. Some don't find it at all, at school or at home, so they might join clubs, groups and even gangs trying to find that deeper feeling of bonding.

The heart smart way to make deeper connections with other people is to first connect deeper within yourself. Remember, this starts with listening to your own heart, your inner security station. When you feel secure in your heart, you can relate to people better.

You feel more connected to them and can understand them at deeper levels. When teens make efforts to understand each other from the heart, it creates the kind of bonding that best friends experience. Relating to people from the heart level can be nurturing and adds energy to the relationship. Surface-level relationships, on the other hand, can leave you feeling drained and unfulfilled.

Bonding gets deeper as you practice relating to others with more sincerity and more care. Practice caring from the heart and treating people the way you want to be treated. See if this doesn't create a deeper connection—and often real fast.

It's important to try to establish a deeper bonding with your parents, or other important adults in your life. In some cases it's hard to do, but it's way worth the effort to try to understand them and their pressures. As you use your heart smarts to understand adults more deeply, it creates more possibilities for bonding and trust. If adults don't respond from their hearts, you can save yourself from a lot of stress by maintaining a non-judging attitude while staying secure inside your heart. Non-judging allows you to feel good with who you are. It keeps your heart from shutting down so you can go on to build positive, bonding relationships with new friends.

As you learn to hear and follow heart directives, you can flow much more smoothly through the challenging times of your life and later turn your challenges into that **inner strength** and success. It takes practice but practice will produce hope. Hope is what the "whole town" is looking for, wouldn't you say?! Give it to them by discovering it within yourself, because you are your own power plant just waiting to be accessed. Remember, don't waste time comparing your life to others who seem more fortunate. Being fortunate is based on how much peace you have, not how many luxuries or conveniences you have. Practice from the heart to make peace with what is, then life gives you more help to change things for the better. You are as good as anyone else, even if you haven't realized it yet. Trust me on this one. You are good and you *can do*. Crank up the heart power and prove me right. Your Buddy.

Poor Me's
Only Mismanaged Emotions

Have you ever felt like you had been totally misunderstood in a certain situation and felt justified in your negative attitude? Here's an example from a friend:

"I had a final paper in sophomore English on the subject of Shakespeare. We were studying *Romeo and Juliet* and I loved the play, the characters, the language, everything. I decided to write the best report on that play ever. I spent the entire semester putting love, care and loads of fun into practically writing a booklet on what was now my favorite subject in school. I created, in my opinion, the best thing I'd ever written. The morning came for my graded paper to come back. Here was the moment I'd been waiting for. My anticipation was high as my teacher returned it to me. I was instantly riveted as I saw the *low* grade due to grammatical errors. She obviously ignored the content and the pure love I put into the project. Guess how I felt? I felt really bad."

How would you feel if something like that happened to you? Angry? Frustrated? Hurt? Resentful? This friend felt all of these feelings and more until about mid-afternoon. These negative emotions are what could be called the legal "poor-me's" or, in a single phrase: "Oh, woe is me, I've been dealt a dirty blow by life!" No matter how justified these emotions seem to be, what do you think happens to your system when you give in to these negative feelings of hurt, anger, resentment and so forth?

Referring back to the computer analogy, these negative emotions can cause a "crash" in your system, similar to putting the wrong access code in your computer. When your computer crashes, you can lose all the data that has been input so far and then you have to redo your data entry all over again. This example works similarly in the human system. After thinking and feeling these "poor-me" reactions, your system can feel debilitated, tired, depressed and totally drained. All of your energy is wasted in these negative emotions and you can find yourself saying, "Here it goes all over again." What do you feel like after you lock yourself in your room, cry, pound the walls, get angry at your teacher, and scream that life isn't fair?...You get the picture. (That's *stinking thinking*). Not too good, huh?

So is this particular state worth these justified emotions? No. They certainly didn't make my friend feel any better. And, believe me, she wished she'd known the hows and whys of controlling her emotions *long before* she turned in that Shakespeare paper. So what would a *heart smart* person say? She could say, "Well, how do I change my feelings when a situation like that is obviously unfair?" One thing that helps is to be consciously aware when an obvious "poor-me" situation comes up, and try to catch the reaction before it gets out of hand (or heart, in this analogy). That's the first step. The next step is quieting down, to cool off and neutralize your reactions. Then you can get a wider view of the exact situation. In this case, my friend had to ask herself, "Will this one paper make or break my school career?" Well, it didn't destroy hers! After all, it was one paper out of one class in all of her years of education.

So, in situations like this you have a decision to make. Is it truly worth all that time and energy feeling bad? Taking a moment to cool off can be a lifesaver because it can save you from those puffy cried-out eyes, a breakout of pimples the next day or that feeling that you just want to eat whatever is in sight. It also helps in

**This kind of thinking never gets anywhere...
I need to start using my own *heart smarts*!**

the long run, because stress builds up in your system and, in some cases, causes all kinds of problems later on down the road. So after you've chilled out and realized that negative emotions can take a toll on your system, leaving you drained and depressed, you will be ready to go to your heart computer for your next readout.

My friend had to realize that it was possible that her teacher might *never* truly understand the dedication and love she put into that paper. When you feel misunderstood, you might get some understanding if you go and talk to the person, but you may never feel completely heard or understood. So what choices do you have?

A *head* choice would be to reenact the scene in your mind, over and over, bringing up potential feelings of resentment and an unforgiving attitude toward the person who misunderstands you. A *heart* choice would be to say, "Well, that's that. I might never be understood so I might as well make the best of it and choose a more efficient way to react in my own system." As a matter of fact, in this situation, my friend eventually came to the conclusion that she had to stay neutral, otherwise she'd have eaten her way into the fat farm. She told herself that the teacher just didn't understand. After all, the teacher didn't know the extent of the dedication she put into the paper and she couldn't blame her for that. My friend wanted to get back the good feeling she had about the class and she liked remembering all the fun she had when she researched and wrote the paper, so she forgave her teacher. Forgiving someone from the heart actually stores positive energy in your system. Most people think that they are doing somebody a favor when they forgive them. Just realize you're doing *yourself* just as big a favor because you dismiss that *stinking thinking* and resentment from your own system. That's getting your head and your heart working together!

For instance, my friend had a concert to go to the night she got her paper back and was going with someone she really cared about. If she hadn't stopped those negative emotions and kept running the gamut of feeling bad, that probably would have put a damper on the whole evening. Her date would have felt the effects of her unhappy or energy-less persona, not to mention her having to conceal puffy eyes and feeling bloated from overeating. My friend did control her emotions, cooled off, and got a wider point-of-view. Then she forgave her teacher, was free of negative emotions, and behaved in a mature way. It released a feeling of enhanced self-esteem. Yes!! She had the full benefit of the night out at the concert and a sparkling night with her date. He might have felt the effects of her enhanced self-esteem through the radiation of her happy feelings because he sure seemed attracted to her positive energy.

See, it's all in the way we view situations, from the heart or the head first. It's up to you, to all of us, because we have the power to change our own systems daily. Try it! It makes streetsense. Become your true self. Take back your own control!

Getting a Grip

Life for me has been a swirl of feelings.
One moment feeling great, then the next I was reeling!
Mad or sad inside — where's that great feeling gone?
I wondered and pondered, and I thought for so long.

I found no answer, until one day I did see
A friend who said, "Please stop, and just be a friend to me!"
(That's how a *true* friend can be, do you see?)
If you love and listen, a buddy's words can be a key.

"Hey, it's *you* who controls the way that you feel.
It's up to you — whether you rock, or you reel!
Hey, it's *you* who controls your own radio show!
That power's within you — that much I do know."

When he said the word "radio," then I could see
That a feeling is nothing but a frequency. (Can that be?)
If I can tune into rock music, or whatever I like,
Then, guess what? I can rock, rock, rock tonight!
But, how about tomorrow, when things aren't so bright?

Ah! Where're those control knobs, I'm ready to start!
My friend said, "Chill out, pal, and start with your heart!
Let your *heart* receive a signal or two,
Then, *use* your heart, to control what you do.

Now, when things happen, I don't just hang there and *feel,*
I tune into my heart first — it's a much better deal!
If I'm sad, I tune into what's funny and smile.
If I'm worried, I change stations and chill out for a while!

Heart control takes practice, but I'm getting it down.
I won't let those feelings drag me all over town!
I don't battle them now, like some guy playing hockey —
Because inside I'm cool — I'm just my own disc jockey!

— *written by a friend*

Self Discovery

5

Pump It Up

Inner Strength

Do you ever remember feeling good when you finally accomplished a certain something you really wanted to do? That feeling is self-esteem, glowing inside. Sometimes, you can have a not-so-good feeling, when you fall off track and *don't* complete what you set out to do. When that happens, you have a choice in how you react. One choice is to feel discouraged and just try to forget you fell into that same old habit again, "Oh well, I don't care anyway." Another choice is to *encourage yourself* and try again. To get that glow inside, it's worth another try!

When you were a kid, you might have heard your mom say to practice your musical instrument. So here we go again talking about having to practice something. You might want to say, "Practice for what? Sometimes I just want to do what I want to do." So here's where you have to realize that what you do is really up to you now.

That's because you have to want something for yourself before you will ever have the power to go for it. This is called desire. Desire is like gas to a car. It will get you where you want to go but first you have to step on the gas pedal. Picking up your foot and putting it on the gas pedal is practice. To be a good driver, you have to practice. The football hero has to practice to be good. He wasn't born with a football in his hand! He learned the rules of the game and practiced. Practicing leads to self-esteem.

Deep in your own heart, you would know if you really want to be something more than a puppet to the world's influences. You know, that feeling inside saying, "I just want to be me." But how? A good place to start is to understand that growing up as a teenager, you become responsible for your choices and your actions. Being young and maybe fairly new to the job of being responsible for yourself makes it harder than you think sometimes. But learning *heart smarts* now during the teenage transition, with your own heart intelligence making balanced decisions with the power to follow through with them — what a headstart on life you would have!

So go to your heart (that place inside where you talk to yourself) and ask, "Is this what I truly want? Is this the most efficient action for me?" Sure, it's a challenge, but you can do it! And the more you do it, the more that good feeling inside starts to grow. That good feeling comes from your heart checking out what's really right for you in any situation. If it leads to something that doesn't feel so good, go back to your heart computer and practice again. Once you add up several of those good feelings, it starts to feel like inner strength developing and not just a lucky day with yourself. That's when you begin to really feel secure from within yourself. That is self-esteem — being a heart smart teenager. Now **there**'s a good accomplishment.

It's just as simple as learning how to swim! You swim lap after lap and you get good at it! Keep making decisions that feel good to you, then follow through with them. Practice! You're building muscles that will make you strong — strong enough to do, or be, or have whatever you want in life. But don't forget that we're talking about heart muscles! True strength comes from the heart. If you have the strength to keep checking in with your heart, really hearing what it has to say, then applying it, you will be doing what's right for you. Not only that,

Inner strength...I'm going for it!

but it keeps feeling better, too! You might end up saying, "I never thought I'd be on the swim team. I did it!"

Believe me, the power to be your own self, to follow your own heart, isn't something you might think is all that important. Rethink that, please! Just imagine starting your life's journey being yourself and really heart smart. It's just plain smart thinking! Need an example? Try this one on. All the kids at a party go with the idea of doing whatever everybody else does all night. "Oh no," you say, "Here it comes — another lecture!" It doesn't have to be that way! Check in with your heart to set up a balance of what might be right for you and really stick to it! Following the crowd has its moments, right? But standing up strong and having a different stroke with self-esteem has its lasting moments! Not only do you build even more of that power, it starts to show! Showing off isn't the point here, but radiating your own strength, on your own, just has to say more than any words. There's something to the old saying, "Actions speak louder than words!" People might make fun of this, but it would be because inside they feel weaker, not stronger, and they might strike out at you.

This is important here. I hope you hear me. Those people that laugh — please don't judge them or think you're better. If you really like this whole idea of gaining inner growth, don't stop here. To have your own power to do what you want to do, you first have to have the power to understand and forgive people that don't. That's real power that nobody can take away from you! You do what you do because it checks out in your heart and feels good to you, not because it pleases the crowd.

What's something your friends do that you're not

comfortable with? Think of a time when you took a different road and stood up strong. How did you feel? But remember, the crowd will never respect you or be able to see you for what you are if you treat them without respect for their choices. The choices you make are yours. Stand up for them. Share them, if somebody wants to listen. But please don't judge anybody for whatever they do. They're doing the best that they have developed the inner strength to do. Doing what's right for you is the very best you can ever do to help or show anybody how to help themselves. Don't worry if sometimes it feels good at first and then later doesn't. Just go back for a heart checkout and then adjust your program again. That's how you keep on discovering what's right for you while accumulating the magic of self-esteem. That can give you the best fun ride through life.

Practice this stuff, get good at it. Then you'll have your own heart experience in getting solutions to problems. Practicing creates the power to deal with whatever comes to you. Inner strength has ways of proving to you, day-by-day, that growing *inside* first can make "growing up" much more fun! The magic of self-esteem is the reward of such practice. Grow with it and go for it!

The Ultimate Dream

Self-esteem
is the ultimate dream.
It makes life full
of the ultimate gleam.
It *is* your deepest heart's true gift,
if you care for others
and you make that shift —
from the analyzing,
categorizing,
processing
head,
to the deepest core heart
that you feel instead.

The real payoff —
life's true essence —
when you really get smart
will give you streetsense.
Your heart's right there
to give you what you need.
Just listen real deeply
and you'll get the seed.

So the fun in life
is up to you now.
Be your own buddy —
your dream-come-true, wow!
The ultimate you
is just waiting to be.
Keep your heart open —
self-esteem is the key.
And that *is* to be.
— Just me!!

— written by a friend

Self Discovery
6

Self-Esteem
A Winning Theme

Very few people feel they have complete self-esteem in all areas of life, but *everybody* wishes they did. A lot of times, popular kids in school seem like they have tremendous amounts of self-esteem. But they might only have it in school in just one area, like in football, or debate, or music. Still, they can have lots of insecurities and problems with their jobs, parents, friends, etc. Self-esteem doesn't exist in the areas where you have insecurities.

To get self-esteem, you first have to start loving yourself and believing in yourself. Try not to take your mistakes in life so seriously. Rather, try viewing mistakes as part of the *adventure* in life or as learning experiences. There are many true stories about successful people who failed over and over but kept trying. They didn't care how many times they made mistakes or failed. Some of them even admit that they may fail again in the future but they'll keep on going no matter what, because they no longer fear failure. They have enough self-esteem to view failure as part of the puzzle and adventure in life, and an opportunity to learn and grow! For example, you are anxious all week about asking someone for a date. You ask and receive a "No... (Crash!) Thank you." Head processing can cause suffering from ego deflation and rejection. Heart thinking gives you the strength to "release and let it go." Don't make a big deal of it. Pick up and move on. Don't box yourself in so that your happiness depends on other people's approval or attention. Operating from the heart is the *bailout.*

Self-esteem comes from making peace with obstacles, while in a fun and excited way figuring out how to overcome them. For example, a guy could try out for the football team and fail. Let's say he decided to stay in his heart and make peace with it, not caring whether he was on the team or not. Then, two months later, a player transferred to a different school, leaving an opening on the team. He was asked to be the replacement. Along the way, he had learned how to have security on the inside, through practicing the smarts of the heart. Later, when he was on the team, it was a fun and exciting *add-on,* yet without it he still had his security so nothing could be taken away. And, he learned that if you don't take chances in life, you can never develop your self-esteem!

As you understand that nobody is better than anyone else, but everyone is unique, then you can see that everyone has many opportunities in life for Self-Discovery — to progress and gain greater fun, peace, adventure and happiness. Think of an area in your life that's difficult or a challenge for you. View it as an adventure! Try making peace with whatever comes your way in life on a consistent basis. You won't be knocked around by life so much when things seem rough and rocky. It's an attitude of understanding that gives you power so you'll be able to keep your peace through the lumps and bumps, and go on. You'll begin to have more confidence in yourself and not compare yourself to others. You'll understand that everyone has their own path to follow in life that is unique and different from anyone else's. Don't judge or envy anyone else's shoes. Just learn to get the most out of the ones on your feet. It cuts stress!

You can play games with yourself. For example, if you have a disagreement or misunderstanding with your parents, instead of getting angry or upset or feeling hurt, you could practice staying balanced and in your heart. Don't lose your good mood but just try loving them and understanding what they are trying to say. Try not to judge them for having their opinions. Doing this on a consistent basis will give you a feeling of greater strength and self-esteem. Even if the points you make don't change their minds, they will see you are more mature and maybe they'll try to listen more deeply to you. You will feel a greater sense of peace within yourself, which gives you a greater sense of strength and self-esteem!

Hey, whatever life brings me, I keep practicing making peace with it. I try to care for myself and others. It really helps so that I don't get so knocked off-balance by what other people do or think! I'm learning to try to clear out negative thoughts or feelings when they come up. That way I build up my own inner security so that whatever comes up is just part of the adventure of life!

You can do it, too! If something seems good, you can just appreciate that it came your way; and if it seems not-so-good, you can just make peace with it, therefore building the power to change what you can. It may sound too simple! By practicing it on a consistent basis I'll bet you'll find that the not-so-good situations seem to resolve themselves in many cases. They'll seem to get better faster than they used to! Each moment you practice in life, you'll be building a giant reservoir of confidence and self-esteem. Then you will have more capacity to help others, which I find to be the most fun and fulfilling adventure of all. Self-confidence is like having a free charge card to the fun events in life. Apply now!

Self Discovery

7

Judgments

Inefficient Investments

Let's talk about judgments and security and how they go together. As I've learned to find security within myself, I have seen that I don't have to judge people anymore. In fact, judging others is an inefficient way to spend energy. When I used to feel insecure, I would compare myself to others and I would tend to judge other people's actions to make myself feel better. It didn't really work. Here's an example of what I mean, from another friend:

"One night I was playing a video game with a friend. I was blasted and realized I had no more players left. However, my friend was still playing with a good life supply left. I felt insecure and thought, 'Oh, he's better than I am and I never get as far as he does.' From that point on, I started to criticize my friend for dumb playing moves. I'd really rub it in and try to discourage him whenever he'd lose a life. Without even knowing it, I was judging my friend. This was because I knew he was better at the game than I was and I felt insecure about it. So I was really taking my insecure feelings out on my friend. I didn't realize that he might feel bad or that I was probably taking the fun out of playing games to-gether. That sure wasn't what I wanted to do. I really wasn't seeing the effect my words were having on him. What's more, I went home not feeling very well. Instead I could have understood, 'Hey, that's my buddy and I'm glad he plays better than I do.' But I needed to feel my own security *first* to realize that."

I asked my friend to tell the same story again, and how he would handle that game now that he knows more about security. Sometimes you do get insecurity attacks, and this is what you can do. So here it goes. Please try to keep an open mind and have fun reading this:

"I was blasted and out of players, but my friend had a good supply of life left. I realized my game was over, even though he was still playing and having a good time. I knew even though I'd lost, that I'd tried my hardest, which was the best I could do. So I stood by my friend, watching over his game. I complimented his good moves instead of criticizing his bad ones. This way it was more fun for my friend and for me, too. He didn't have to worry about whether I cared about losing or not. I forgot about losing and really got into the excitement of him playing, as if I were playing right there with him. After the game, I told him what a great game he had played. I also asked him if maybe he would help me learn some better game strategies and moves. He said, 'Yeah, sure!' Then we both walked away feeling great and both of us had a really good time!"

Sounds like two people riding off into the sunset at the end of a movie, huh? The reason the second story worked out this way is simple. By knowing inside yourself that you tried hard and did your best, you feel an inner security. You may not be as experienced as your friend, but you're pretty darn good yourself! So you can see that judging other people and feeling a lack of inner security is a waste of energy! It would be a more effi-

Less judgments = more FUN !

cient use of your energy to know that you are the best person you can be, and know you always try your best no matter what the situation may be. Realizing this more often will give you a build-up of inner security, and things will probably tend to flow more smoothly. Situations that usually seem very difficult may seem better. Then it's easier to make it through without having to try as hard as you used to.

Remember, judgments are an inefficient investment of your energy. Why waste energy on something that only brings less security and less fun? As you learn to access your heart computer — especially at times when it would be easy to judge someone — you'll find efficient options that can build more inner security. (We'll talk more about this in the next chapter.)

So, basically, what I'm trying to tell you as a friend is that by not judging and by always keeping your own inner security, you may be a happier person and have more fun!

Care
An Enrichment for Self-Esteem

Life can be wonderful if you allow your heart to be your *best buddy;* it can be the best you will ever have. In understanding that, it could make all the difference between a happy life or a sad life. It's really pretty simple. What it means is, "Are you using your own energies efficiently or inefficiently?" Energies are what run the emotional, mental and physical aspects of your system — you. Learning to control and balance the energies in your own system right in the middle of everyday situations makes life user-friendly. It is the gateway to new beginnings of what life can bring to you.

Let's look at your whole being again as a computer system, with the heart as the master controller. Through the heart comes the *control and balance* we're talking about. The heart is your key to a whole new world full of stimulation — joy, peace and just true fun every day. Isn't that what you would want a best buddy to give you? Now, how do you get this key, this experience of the heart? There are some programs that can activate the master controller of your computer. The first one is *caring*.

Caring for people is one of life's puzzles that, when you solve it, has a big surprise built-in. Let's talk more deeply about this one. True caring is a heart response to life. In caring, you activate the heart to feel and actively put out heart feelings. Heart feelings are powerful. To understand how powerful they truly are, right now, try remembering how it feels to be really happy versus very sad. Even in the middle of a disagreement with your mom or dad or best friend, I know and you know, you still love them. To remember that at the time is *caring*. It could leave you laughing at the end of the disagreement and having fun instead of not speaking.

Caring from the heart creates a powerful and magnetic energy field around you that can start to draw to you more fun and harmony in life. Life has lots of gifts and *stands on go* waiting for the right time to send them your way. What's more, these gifts, like stimulation, joy, love and fun surprises, are specially designed just for you. Life does want you to have fun, like that laugh with a friend. Life is designed for self-discovery and growth. Growing up on the inside means learning how to run your system efficiently to produce fun on the outside. Maybe that is what life is really about, waiting for everyone to get heart smart enough to discover the surprises that come from true caring. All else might be sidelines that take you through the maze until you can get your priorities straight. The route through the maze is true caring put into action.

"Caring for people" might remind you of Sunday school, but it wouldn't be smart to judge too quickly. Don't you like to be loved, cared for and liked? True care for people makes sense because it brings results you like, but you can only know that by doing it. People who practice real heart care find it much more profitable to them than all the money in the world. Money would be no fun if everyone disliked you. Putting your real heart first brings you care and then money is an *add-on*. This might sound sweet, but it is streetsense. That's how your heart computer works.

In everyday life, situations always come up where you have to make a choice of how you respond. If you judge the situation or you judge another person, you are activating the feeling of judgment through your system. You are actually taking on the attitude that you *know* what he or she should or shouldn't do. Try to really feel this from the heart. Judgment separates you from the person. It cuts off your caring. It's an inefficient use of your energies.

It's hard not to judge. Sometimes you will just be assessing something and you find it turns into a judgment. But how do you know what you would have done in any given situation, unless you are standing completely in that person's shoes? Caring would be having compassion for what it must be like to be in their shoes. No human being has the right to judge another, mainly because you can never know completely what it's like to be that person. So if you start to feel yourself judging, switch to caring — that heart feeling — and see what gifts unfold.

Judgments are tricky. They pop up automatically. Practice catching yourself judging someone and consciously shift your focus to a heart attitude. The head tends to judge but as you shift to the heart, you will learn to release the judgments and replace them with compassion. It takes practice, yet what doesn't if you want to achieve any measure of success (musical instruments, golf, tennis, dance, etc.)? Hey, it's *way* worth the practice just to clear *stinking thinking* out of your system.

I was once in a situation where all the kids in the class were razzing the substitute teacher. She was trembling and looked like she didn't know what to do. Ordinarily I would have judged her as a flake and kept laughing. But, I decided to practice compassion and that let me see she was embarrassed and maybe about to cry. I don't think I would have noticed that if I'd kept on laughing along with the others. By activating that feeling of compassion for someone, I really got a deeper understanding of what it must feel like to be in her shoes. This help comes from the heart. Judgments come from the head and only add negative energy both to the situation and to your system. To add to the negativity can feel good in the moment, but negativity feeds back on you somewhere else, mentally, emotionally or physically. True care is just loving someone quietly through the hard times. Sometimes that is the best you can do. On an energy level, people get your positive energy and that positive energy comes back to you somewhere else. The planet is starving for positive energy, so let's feed it something healthy for a change.

I have practiced caring from my heart with compassion in day-to-day situations. It proved to me that judgments were a very inefficient use of my energy. They don't make for any fun or good results. As you practice, you come to understand how it all works. Compassion for a person takes you to what's called an *overview*. That's when you a get a wider picture of what's really going on. Maybe you don't get a complete understanding, but at least you see that people are functioning to the degree that they have practiced self-management. In that understanding alone, you adapt more peacefully to the situation and save yourself from a lot of stress. It can even give you creative direction on how to really help. Think of someone you've judged and try to really feel compassion for them for a few minutes. It may feel awkward the first few times but so is your first attempt to ride a bike. The practice will bring positive results, especially when you start to feel better about yourself. Feeling better about yourself is self-esteem.

Look at it like black and white. To judge somebody for whatever they do is just not smart use of energy on any level. Let life judge and sentence people, for it has a sophisticated system with balanced overview to take care of such matters. Make a fun project of learning to manage your own energies and true self-esteem will be the reward. With a little effort, you will soon start to experience new shades of happiness. Think of what a tonic the planet would receive if people were as concerned about what they think and feel as much as they are concerned about what they eat and how they look. It's legal to be concerned about your physical aspects but it's possible that people need to be more attentive to their thinking process and emotional management. Without that, you could have perfect physical health and still be a long way from experiencing peace. Yes, a long way. It's especially good to learn heart smarts while you are young so you won't have to unlearn so much later in life. Growth is not so much the new habits we have to learn, it's the undoing of the wrong habits we have developed and live by.

Sincere care for people is a smart use of your energies, a very wise investment in the game of life. Remember the equation — what you put out, you get back. The more care you put into your life, the more life will care for you, bringing you fun adventures, great friends, and real inner security. Caring is just good streetsense.

So,   Judge less
        and unstress,
        Care more
        and high score.

Buddies
Through Thick and Thin

Now here's a subject, "buddies," that ought to touch everybody a little in the heart. Tune into your heart computer right now and hear this — my experience is that buddies are worth way more than all the gold on the planet. But what is a buddy? It's simple — a true friend from the heart. Buddies don't find each other from the head. Only deep in the heart can a true friend be made. A heart-to-heart buddy is one of the best things life has to offer. It's that bond you feel with a really close friend who you can tell anything to — tell stories about last night's date, talk on the phone for hours, talk about teachers, laugh about good times and just basically kick back, being yourself.

Being true buddies takes a lot of love — the kind of love that doesn't change if your buddy changes. Loving someone for just being themselves isn't always easy. People seem to want others to be and do what they want them to be and do. However, in growing friendships people do change a lot, and true buddies are always there for each other. How do you do it? How can you be there for your buddies even when you are going different ways?

People will always grow and move on in life. Your buddies now may not be the same ones who were your best buddies when you were in kindergarten. In the heart, you can always be in touch with someone you care about. Caring is the real meaning of friendship. It's not what you can get out of someone, but rather, what you can put in that builds friendship. True feelings of care mean just wanting someone to be all right and given

Whether sharing a sunset or enjoying a good party, there's nothing like a true buddy in life.

the best chances in life. That's the best thing you could want for your buddy. Now, you invest this kind of love into people and you're just likely to get back a lot of true buddies who are there for you all along the way, too. So remember, you can never have too many buddies in life. The more the merrier! The more buddies, the more people to have fun with.

A great advantage of a true buddy is that they will give you feedback that you need to hear, not just what you want to hear. There's nothing like having a buddy to practice heart smarts with. When one of you is stuck in the head and obviously not operating from the heart, the other can remind him. It can be fun sharing with each other that way and it helps speed you along towards self-management. Having a friend that truly understands is that gold I'm talking about.

Loving someone doesn't mean they always love you back. So you just love them for being themselves and go on with life. That may seem hard to do, but it's worth it. If you keep your heart open, your friendships won't get sticky. Life offers lots of people for you to love. It's important to remember to always appreciate them for the gifts that they are. This appreciation just helps you remember how lucky you are to have good buddies, even if it's just one or two at any given time.

Good buddies are worth working for. Working for means to remember that your friendship is worth so much more than silly differences. Remember, true buddies are buddies through thick and thin, not just when things are going great. It's really easy. Just love your friends and always be the best buddy you can be. That's one of life's puzzles that is so simple, but the return is so great!

With or Without
Being Wise in Relationships

The love relationships that really last are the ones in which you become real buddies first, or at least along the way. The sweetheart phase is what it is — a phase — with novelty and romance. People love that high-powered emotional feeling, but it can also be a real roller coaster ride that leaves you wondering if it's really worth it. When you build the relationship out of true friendship, you put a solid ramp under the whole thing. The ramp doesn't take the adventure out of the ride — it makes it more secure and fun.

A special relationship with someone at any age is always going to be full of challenges. Challenges dealt with through the heart computer can take you to even better, deeper feelings than what you've already had. Before we go even a little further, what about the challenges of not having a special person in your life? There are challenges when you don't have someone, as well as when you do have someone. One way or the other, challenge is always going to be there. Life brings you, at different periods, chances to make the most out of either situation so you can try to grow stronger in the heart. So whether you're with someone or alone, you can almost talk about both experiences side by side. It's really the same kind of inner self-discovery you have to do in order to find out what's the best for you. Sound a little strange?

Take the example of two people who are at the point of their relationship where it's not in the first fun, novelty stages any more. Differences start to come up, like concerns about ownership of each other, along with just plain old lumps and bumps. What do they do now? Well, at this point most people fuss and fight and decide that they don't love each other any more and go their separate ways. But remember, we talked about being buddies first and what a foundation that can build. Finding a friend and giving your friendship all the heart you can is, again, one of the most important investments you will ever make in life. Then if you do part your ways, it can be peaceful — still friends.

People feel that investing deep heart care causes them to be vulnerable, to getting walked on and hurt. Guess what? It's the other way around. It's your deep heart that picks you back up after your mind made you vulnerable to people by having too many expectations of them. In your deep heart, you can be vulnerable but not threatened. The threats seem like they come from the heart, yet it's the head that sets you up to be hurt in relationships, such as: idealistic expectations; basing your happiness on someone else's actions or opinions; jealousy because of not having built your own self-security; seeking happiness through *wanting* rather than giving, etc. That's all head stuff. There is some heart mixed in it, but not the matured, self-secured, deep heart. The intention of this book is to help facilitate your development of that kind of deeper heart.

After you establish deep heart maturity, then relationships can add to you but can't take a lot away from you. In your heart you probably would really want to be solid and secure in your own power and not have to depend on other people's "batteries." Ha! That's just streetsense.

So what do you do if your relationship starts to go wrong? Go back to the heart and remember that you just love that person. You don't own them, you just love them. Loving someone and appreciating them for being themselves is the buddy foundation you are building for deeper friendship and better times.

Learning to love someone without expectations about what they do or don't do is one of the hottest keys to gaining your own heart security. Now you might be thinking, "How will I ever get what I want if I don't have expectations?" By going for your own heart security, life is more likely to give you what you really do want. Your heart security is a gift life wants you to have any way it can give it to you — that's why the challenges come up. Heart security — the power to love someone with or without that love coming back the way you might want it to — is real *heart power* in action.

Take another example of two people, the first one is in a relationship, the second isn't. The first says, "If I could just get out of this relationship, it would be the best thing that ever happened to me!" The second is saying, "If I could just find someone, it would be the best thing that ever happened to me!" So around and around we go, with or without a relationship. Whichever side, it's up to you to make the changes in your life that make the difference between having heart security or not.

So whether you have a partner or not, heart security is challenged both ways. This is just life helping to make you go deeper in your own heart to find true peace and be happy. It's up to you if you want to take these challenges and go for it. Happiness really is born from within yourself, not from the outside world around you. Find or develop your own heart security first, then whatever life brings to you is an add-on but not a take-away. Nobody can truly make you happy if you're not happy with yourself first. If you are happy with yourself, then if someone comes along it can be the truly fun add-on in life that a relationship is meant to be.

The heart is your truest buddy, waiting to guide you in a fun way, not the way of misery. You can give a relationship all you have from the heart and not hold on to the old ways of ownership, possessiveness and jealousy. Believe me, feelings like that only push people further apart, never closer together. Only when two people are secure in their own hearts can they bond more deeply and closely together. Put that kind of bonding between two people and you might find out what a "match made in heaven" is all about. So, whether you're with someone or not, don't put the cart in front of the horse. Go for your own growth, your own heart power first, and take on life as the fun adventure it's meant to be.

In short, be wise and build a solid relationship with yourself first. Then, other relationships have a better chance for success — a tip from the Doc.

Let's Talk
It Cleans Stinking Thinking

Communication can seem so complicated sometimes, but it really can be a simple process. When communicating, you send out a message or idea, and then someone receives it. One of the things that can complicate the communication process is the emotionalism that often comes through with the message. For lots of people, emotions are hard to keep under control. Sometimes, people can *seem* totally chilled out, but the next minute they explode like a nuclear bomb!

What causes those screaming outbursts? One of the main causes is that people often let things build up without saying how they feel. After a while, you can get to a point where you feel like, "Man, this is gettin' out of hand!"

Here's an example from when I was first starting to use my heart computer as a teenager. (Unfortunately, in this case, my head computer was still running the show.) One day I came home from school and saw my sister wearing one of my shirts. When she saw me, she said, "Oh, I wanted to wear this to that party tonight — you don't mind, do you?" Out loud, I said, "No, go ahead." But, inside, I really wished she would have asked me first. Over the next few weeks, the same thing happened five more times, and I always said, "Go ahead," but felt differently inside. Why do girls like to wear guys' clothes anyway?! My head processors were building the case. I was ill. Finally, one day, she walked in my room, and started fishing through my clothes. I couldn't stand it anymore so I yelled, "How dare you come in and start grabbing my clothes! You never even ask before you use my things!" My sister stared at me in shock, then burst into tears and ran from the room. In that moment, I felt

It's better to talk it out than to blow up and pop!

terrible about how I had yelled at her, and that was *worse* than feeling irritated about her taking my clothes!

This is an example of the buildup problem that happens when you don't communicate how you really feel about something from the start. To beat the problem, have the philosophy of "communicate as you go, don't wait 'til you blow." It makes sense — it's like doing regular maintenance on your car so the engine doesn't blow up! In the example above, I could have saved the blowup by telling my sister, the very *first* time she borrowed something, that I would really appreciate it if she asked me first. How else would she really know that was my preference if I didn't *tell* her? It would have been easy for me to feel kind of stupid for taking so long to see that I obviously needed to communicate my feelings earlier. But, I tuned into my heart computer and realized, "Oh, well — I really missed that one, but I'm sure not perfect and at least I got to learn something new about how communication works! Now, I'll just decide what would be the best thing to do next!"

Lots of times, we avoid telling someone the truth because we are afraid that the person won't like what we're about to say. In the example above, I thought, "If I tell my sister to ask before she borrows, she'll get mad at me, or say I'm selfish — it is easier just to say nothing." It's really *not* easier, I found out, because all those unsaid things built up until I blew up, and then I had a lot of extra work to do. I had to struggle to get my emotions back in control, then find a way to talk with my sister about the borrowing process so she understood why I blew up. See? I had to tell my truth anyway, *and* clean up the mess caused by the blowup.

Try to see communicating your own truth as something positive. I know that I would rather have someone tell me the truth than to have them dislike me or snub me, without me even knowing why. If I just remember how I would want to be spoken to, that helps me to *communicate from my heart* to another person, sincerely wanting us to understand each other.

When you sincerely practice communicating from the heart, you'll notice you will have fewer fears about how someone might react to whatever you say. Instead of worrying, "She'll get mad at me, she'll think I'm being mean," you might think of it this way: Did you ever notice how *glad* someone is when you tell them they have a piece of spinach sticking to their front teeth? For a second, they are embarrassed, but then they *thank* you for pointing it out — that's what true friends and buddies do for each other! Really, if my sister appreciated borrowing my shirt and hoped she could borrow more clothes in the future, she would be happy to know how to do the one thing that would make me feel good about it — just asking me first. Telling her that would be a favor to her *and* to me. Stay clear as you go. It keeps the static build-up out of your face — a lot more fun I assure you. Communication is something you can always practice with your next conversation. How neat — what if most people started mixing a little communication in with their conversations in life. Things would be better, huh? Go for it!!!

Deep Listening
Prevents Deep Trouble

What does "deep heart listening" mean? Or, better yet, a more important question would be, *"How do you do it?"* When someone says, "Listen deeply," they really are saying, "Please hear what I'm trying to say." Now, to really listen and hear is **trickier** than you might think. To start, you might ask yourself to listen deeply to your own heart. Training yourself to listen to, obey, and follow your own heart directives in life is really a big order but it's easier to make progress than you think. The most helpful hint on how to practice would be to ask your heart to help you to listen more deeply. This would be the smart way — "Heart Smarts!"

Listening is a true art. To run a deep listening program, learn to shut off your own thoughts and tune into your own heart or to someone else's. It takes practice. Not many people, I bet, can say they really do that. Listening to others talk to you without running your own mind program at the same time does take control; so does listening to your own heart without your head thoughts distracting you.

When I began accessing my heart computer, I asked myself, how could I really hear someone tell me something about their world or feelings if I was split, half-listening and half-talking to myself inside? I realized as they were talking that I was missing some of what they were trying to say. I was not focused.

If you really *want* to hear what is being said, then you might find yourself *listening deeply*. Deep heart listening is when you quiet some of the head chatter and relax into a more focused-attention listening frequency. Deep heart listening is the other half of true communication, which is speaking your truth from the heart. Now, to listen deeply doesn't mean you have to agree, just that you at least hear it all. When you listen only part way, or interrupt, you can miss a lot of the meaning of someone's words — what their heart is really saying. You still don't have to agree, but if you know you really listened from the heart and heard them, then you truly know what it is you're not agreeing with. Deep heart listening also gives you more power to clearly say what you need to say after you've fully heard someone else. To make it simple, it's just smart to want to hear all, so your own heart computer readout can assess the complete data and then use your head to give the best, balanced response possible. That happens if you listen from the heart. It takes practice.

Deep heart listening is an intelligent asset to have in life. It can not only help you in communicating and in hearing other people, but also in learning to hear yourself. Listening the "heart smart" way is the maximum fun way. Remember to slow down a minute and really check in with your heart computer and ask your heart for the best message to come through. Deep heart listening is a handy program to have to help understand the true feeling of a communication.

Here's an example from a friend's viewpoint of what can happen without deep heart listening:

"My boyfriend and I used to spend time talking all over each other's words, talking about the same thing at the same time and arguing about it. Sounds silly, but *listen deeply*. We would argue forever, it seemed, about our two different points of view. He would say we weren't connecting in the heart very well. I would take off on how hurt I was that he didn't feel my heart. Then he would go on and on about how everything I was doing lately was wrong. I would go on defending myself. He would then say I was proving that what he was saying was right. Oh boy, it could go on for hours. A friend came along and asked, 'What's going on here?' At that point, we were both pretty worn out and very hurt. In trying to explain to the one objective listener, we both found out that all we were saying to start with was how much we loved each other and missed that heart connection if things weren't right. It's wild realizing the maze my head can send me through to find a simple solution."

So, there you have it. Not taking the time to really *listen deeply* from your heart can send you flying in the wrong direction. It happens a lot in life. People just run their own thoughts so hard and fast, they don't stop to truly hear what another is saying (or what their own heart is saying) much of the time. This couple now has a running joke about it since they've caught on. Before they go 'round and 'round in a disagreement, they stop and ask, "What are you really saying," and, "I *promise* I'll listen deeply this time." It's the deeper levels of listening that will really bring the resolutions you wanted in the first place.

Just try to listen completely to what someone is saying and really let them finish their story. Let them finish even if you want to state your point before you forget it. It's more important that the other person feel heard and really understood. If what you wanted to say is important, your heart readout will bring it back sooner or later. So, don't let your head thoughts come in and cut someone off with your own opinions until they truly finish. Then, tell your truth to them

Heart listening really does help you to allow someone to finish talking before you start making mental judgments!

and ask them to try to do the same. This might not solve the problem but you will at least have a better picture of what the whole thing is really about. It's like a ping pong game. It's your time, it's my time.

Remember, you have to listen from your heart. Your heart doesn't judge people for thinking differently. You might not always agree but you keep that bond of friendship.

Here's a *fun how-to game* to help practice *deep heart listening*. When you're talking (or, I should say, listening) to someone, see if you can play, "don't open your mouth" until the other person is finished talking completely. Now, this is the tricky part: Try to keep your inner mind-talk to a minimum. It's natural to have a high speed thought, but then gently go back to focused listening. So, good luck, try it out. But, be smart. Use your heart not only to help you listen to what they're saying; but feel inside that you really want to know. That will help stop the inner chatter and help you practice having the power to *deep heart listen*. It's actually fun to train yourself to listen. Give it a spin and enjoy the humor that accompanies self-study.

Self Discovery
13

Living in Box-ins?
A Way Out

What's a selected perspective? It's how you choose to look at things. If you select the same program all the time as your own view, then you have boxed yourself in. Try selecting a wider view of things. It's fun. Box-ins limit you to being too rigid in a stance, not allowing you to be flexible. You might be seeing things too black or too white, thinking it's either one way or the other with no other variables. Perspectives do expand. That's what teenagers' growing up is about — expanding your perspectives as you go out into the world. Some of your truths as you see them now can and will change. When you are operating from your heart directives, you are free to explore along many lines according to what feels fun and right to you. Try checking out new life experiences, expanding without boxing yourself in. Use your heart computer.

Here's a major stress level that teenagers go through. One day, you are just a teenager bopping along, and then your parents ask, "What are you going to do for the rest of your life?" This is an often played-out scene that has a seemingly twisty or conflicting aspect to it. First you may hear something like, "You're so lucky! You have your whole life ahead of you. You can be absolutely anything you want to be!" Because of wisdom and love, parents really do want to help, but they actually often add pressure to the situation by giving teenagers some strong opinions about what to do. Meanwhile, you're probably wondering, "What *do* I want to be when I grow up? What am I going to study? I don't really know!" Then, the bomb: "The choices you make now are going to affect the rest of your life. You'd better make the right choices!" Frustration can really start building now, since most teenagers just don't know yet.

What a set-up! The funny thing is, each of the statements above has a truth in it. So how do we put our puzzles together without **stress** or confusion as we try to sort out the pieces and find our own perspective? As teenagers, you are at a certain point in life where you are really *lucky,* because you haven't placed yourselves in a box yet. As you learn to use the heart computer, you don't have to box yourself in!

So how do you deal with choices and not put yourself in a box? In that moment when you need to make a choice, *first* choose to go to your heart computer for help, instead of letting the options bounce around in your *head*. Your heart can give you the wider perspective to help your head see the whole situation as it really is. The wider perspective can help guide you to do what would be best for you. It is the head that can make everything a big deal, as it tries to see the future and all the possible things that could go right or wrong. The head can also start to list all the steps you have to go through to achieve a career, making you feel like, "Well, if I want to have that career, I have to choose *now* or I'll never get there!" If that checks out in your wider heart perspective, do it. If not, wait for your heart readout.

I'm glad I found out about the system of going to the heart computer. Now, I have a chance of finding out which is the real me!

When you go to your heart, you get more in touch with the real you. Your heart can help you find and understand the wider perspective that doesn't box you in. It's not wishy-washy. That's the head again, unsure of itself. The heart computer can give you the security that whatever career you choose, that is just *one* part of life, as important as it may be. NO BIG DEAL. These days, many people have two or three careers in their lifetime, not just one. Choose what sounds fun, practical and fulfilling to you now — there will be other times coming to make other choices — then carry them out. And, *have fun* on your career adventure!

The attitude of "No Big Deal" doesn't make the choice unimportant — it helps you stay in balance. A balanced perspective helps fit the pieces of life's puzzle together with more ease and with a lot more fun. So, don't box yourself in with a limited perspective, like thinking this is your one and only chance to do it right. You might make a decision and stick with it. Then again, in three years you might find some other choice that you want more. All of life's choices are like a puzzle. You can have fun or stress with putting the pieces together. It's your choice.

It's not just with career choices that people box themselves in. It's also in day-to-day situations. Here's an experience I once had (as I was first learning to use my heart computer):

On the last study night before finals, one of my friends said, "Who cares?! Let's all forget about school and go to the movies!" At first, my head tried to rationalize with negative thoughts like, "I'm going to fail anyway, I might as well go to the movies," and, "I really need to study, but this is my only chance to see that movie with my friends," and, "My friends won't like me if I don't go." If I had given in to the head thoughts, or the peer pressure, I would have boxed myself in to fail. Instead, I chose to stop those thoughts and take a moment to check my heart computer. My heart told me things like, "I need to make my best effort on those finals," and "I can always see that movie tomorrow night when the test is over," and, "If they're really my friends they'll want me to do my best." My heart also gave me the feel-good energy to carry out my choice. I actually ended up enjoying the movie more at another time, since I didn't have to think about the test at all while I was watching it! The heart computer helps your head not box itself in because the heart gives you the wider, balanced perspective on the future consequences of your choices. It's there to work for you.

Lots of people have stories about how they hurried into a decision to get a certain kind of security that comes from feeling, "Okay, that's settled." Sometimes teenagers make hasty decisions when they are going too fast, such as doing something just to keep up with their buddies or to be cool. The problem is this: by going for that kind of security you could be wrapping yourself so far into a cozy little cocoon, putting yourself in a box, that you may not be free to follow a better idea that comes to your heart. Stress usually results from a conflict between the head and the heart. The head says to go this way, and the heart tells you to go the other way. To settle the conflict, let the head speak, then go to the heart and let the heart speak. Many times the head thoughts seem to be the most stimulating and satisfying *in the moment*. However, after the dust settles, you may be paying a lot of dues because of a quick choice that was made while seeking stimulation. Lead with your heart and your head will follow. That's what it's designed to do. Heart choices bring you balanced stimulation and a feeling that is complete and satisfying to your whole system. Sometimes you can tell what is the highest right in the moment, and sometimes the answer will come a few days later.

If I can just get this energy down to my heart, I'd get out of this box-in and find a solution!!

I'm not saying don't use your head. Use it to gain information so you make informed choices. Use your parents or teachers to gather information. If they give you an opinion about what you should do, then talk to them. Ask them why they feel that way, and you might get a great story about an important choice they made when they were your age. Communication like this widens your perspectives and helps you to make choices. Having the wider perspective helps you fe el secure about the choices you do make. Be yourself. That creates self-security in your own choices. You can be what you are and not be threatened by what someone else is or says. Allow others to have their opinions, respect them and try to understand them. And, remember — it's okay for you to have your own opinions, too. Use your heart computer. It takes practice, but what you gain is worth it!

If you make decisions with your head controlled by your heart, you will have your heart readout to help you know which way to go. Then, only you can choose whether you do it halfway or really **go for it**. The more you can focus on doing your best at something, really putting your whole self into it, the more you will find the self-security that really counts — the confidence, energy and self-esteem that comes from knowing you can do what you set out to do. Doing your best moves you forward in life. Doing things halfway leaves you stuck in that box, looking back and wondering, "What if I *had* done my best?" Choices made from the heart perspective give you the overview to do your best without any stress. That's how I've found success and fun in putting my puzzle together. YOU can do it, too! Try this fun experiment:

Write down a conflict you are struggling with.

Listen to your head (your quick, automatic thoughts). What does it say? Now listen deeply and quietly to your heart. What does it tell you? What choice will you make?

After you practice, you will develop a knack for knowing which is the head and which is the heart. Then the fun starts and the stress is soon on its way out the door. Enjoy!

Why Say No?!
The Real Problem Behind Drugs

This commentary is going to catch you off-guard, possibly. Here's why. You are probably guessing ahead and preparing yourself to be preached to about drugs. You have probably heard about the negative effects of drugs and have been told to "Just Say No," until it is burnt into your brain. Right?

Well, there's nothing wrong with being educated on the subject. That increases your intelligence which increases your power for making heart smart choices. Relax, it's not my intention to give you another lecture on drugs. The problem at hand is deeper than drugs. Drug abuse is only the *symptom*. The *problem* is the lack of true self-esteem within the individuals, especially teenagers. So sometimes it's better to deal with problems by going in the back door rather than the front.

Ponder this — if the planet would wage a "war on stress," then the appetite for drugs would favorably decrease. You see, after kids are told, "Just Say No," there is not a lot offered to replace that emptiness and boredom they experience inside. They turn to drugs and other indulgences for release, then realize later those things make even a bigger mess. Still the problem needs attention.

Now let's talk about the real drug problem: **depression**. Did you know that depression causes the release of negative hormones in your body that act to deteriorate and deplete your system over a period of time? That's what drugs do, too — they change your hormonal patterns leading to depletion, and rapidly so. Drugs may feel good on the ingoing but deplete your system on the outcoming. If depression releases hormones that cause deterioration of your system, then it has a negative self-drug effect. — Help! — Who ya gonna call? **"Stress Busters."** Who is that? YOU! It could be fun to be trained as a *stress buster*. Then you could sneak in the back door and possibly do more for the drug problem on the planet than anyone ever dreamed of. Stress busters build something they can rely on for fun and happiness so they can "say no to drugs."

With the fast pace of life, people have lost contact with the true feeling of the family unit. The education and ambition that teens are taught need to be balanced with teachings about character, self-empowerment and *heart* discrimination (heart smart choices). These Heart Smarts practices need to be the principal subject matter in the curriculum so that the other subjects will have a bottom line to build on. You would be surprised what this would do for the drug problems and other related problems in life. This sounds too simple, but a trained stress buster would know that the magical solutions in life are well hidden in simplicity. Hey, I'm not preaching. You know I wouldn't do that! Ha! I'm just giving you an inside tip at the race track, a secret for winning.

If you become a stress buster while you are a teenager, think of all the frustrations, emotional pains and relationship hassles that you would eliminate while growing into an adult. If you practice now, you don't have to *pay* as much later. By *pay*, I'm talking about all the baggage and luggage of unnecessary built up stress that most people carry with them their whole lives. This whole book has been designed with many helpful hints on how to become a stress buster.

A real STRESS BUSTER uses HEART POWER!!!

Heart power is the tool of the stress buster and the key to the continuous *high* you are looking for in life. Realize you can get a *quick fix* for depression and boredom by releasing the power in your own heart. It takes a little practice and doesn't cause the wear and tear on your body, mind and emotions. In fact, activating heart power causes the release of positive, uplifting hormones in your body. By practicing the heart smart suggestions in this book, you can learn how to "say no to stress." Then you won't need to say yes to drugs. Sure you can't eliminate all stress in life totally, but you can easily do away with the personal overload that's causing most of the teenage problems of today.

Learn to follow the voice in your heart and be surprised at the new frequency of happiness and fun that comes your way. You have your own *caretaker* built in, you just have to learn to communicate with it. The war on drugs will finally have to be won by going within and doing it yourself, not waiting for the government to seize all of the dope. You and I both know that would be a long wait. I know you heard that. It's streetsense, right? Let's declare "war on stress" and cut the drug problem off at the pass. Sounds like a rational approach to me.

So, when problems arise, who ya gonna call?— **Stress Buster!** Right — the magic power of your own heart. Catch you later.

Self
Discovery
15

Music
How It Affects You

Okay, let's talk about music. Most of you probably like music and, hey, that's good. Music is fun! Teenagers usually seem to come in with the new music — kind of like the new rhythm of life. When swing music came along way back in the '40s, it was the teenagers who made it popular; and when the Beatles hit it big it was — guess who? — the teenagers who liked them first. Everybody has their favorite types of songs and their favorite groups. Most of you probably like rock, rap, or good dance stuff. All of these types of music are good and I like a lot of them also! Music is a powerful influence and lots of people are really into it. However, most people don't realize just how much effect it has on them. Music can influence your attitude in life, but that can go both ways: positive or negative. That's because music is a tremendous *frequency carrier*. Every kind of music carries its own unique set of frequencies. Some of these frequencies are better for your system than others and all forms of music can have a strong effect on the listener.

Let's look at music as food for your mental and emotional health. If you don't eat a balanced diet of regular food, it can lead to physical problems. If your mom fed you junk food and sweets all of the time, that might be what tastes best to you. But in the long run, eating that way can lead to health problems. You wouldn't want your mom to do that to you, would you? You can prevent some of these problems by eating a balanced diet from time to time, even if it's not your favorite food. Music works the same way on your mental and emotional nature.

I've been involved in experiments that showed me how hard-driving, loud and aggressive music creates edginess, nervousness and disorientation. It can cause the nervous system to stay keyed up too long at a time without a counter-rhythm of rest and recuperation. This eventually can affect your behavior patterns. It would vary with different people, yet some are more vulnerable because of having a more sensitive nature. Hey! Chill out. Some of you are getting ill at me because it sounds like I am going to attack your favorite musical groove. Let me finish what I'm saying, then you can "clobber" me if it doesn't check out. Okay, I like selections of rock, rap, groove, metal, etc. However, I'm careful to balance that out with some softer classical and contemporary instrumental type music. I'm not suggesting you change from rock to soft music. I'm just saying that the need for a balance could be more important than you think, especially if you listen to high energy, hard-driving music daily. People may tell you it's bad to listen to that kind of music and you probably feel misunderstood. When adults over-preach to teenagers about the rights and wrongs of their musical choices, then teenagers soon lose respect for whatever adults have to say about anything and everything. This is because music is a sensitive subject. And so are teens. In the future, hopefully, teens and adults alike will begin to bridge the gap in communication through the wisdom of the heart, and stop beating their heads against a brick wall. This will eliminate resistance and illuminate understanding. The result would be that teens and adults could bond together as good buddies, while closing the generation gap that is so popular for producing stress.

Remember, music is food, so practice a balanced diet.

Enough philosophy. Let's boogie! I plan to enjoy my rock music from time to time but because of using my heart smarts, I know when to back off, switch frequencies and balance out my nervous system. That's all I'm asking you to consider. I've made records from rock to contemporary instrumental and I will continue to do so. It's fun. I've also studied the effects of music on human sensitivities for many years and that's why I've shared with you the suggestions concerning balance in your musical appetite. It's the extremes that throw your mental and emotional nature out of phase. Too much of anything in life is not the best way to go if fun and fulfillment are what you're looking for.

Here's an experiment: if you are the type that "rocks out" every day (believe me, I used to) check into some calming instrumental music even if you don't like that type. (It's possible to learn to like it. I did.) It serves as a tonic to smooth out the rock and the rap occasionally. Then you can crank up again, yet you'll be heart smart enough to appreciate balance as well. Hey, discover this yourself! Listen to music from your heart and you will develop a true feeling for what type you need and when. See, I wasn't attacking your music after all. Hey, we're Buddies. When you want to rock, just call the Doc. I'm ready.

Appreciation
A Magnetism Overlooked

As I was growing up, my parents always told me to say "please" and "thank you." They told me that I should appreciate everything I was given. Well, I'm more mature now than I was at five. But I'm still learning about appreciation and the good it can do for a person's system.

Sincere appreciation is obviously magical because people and life seem to give you more and more when you really appreciate. "Please" and "thank you" often represent only surface levels of appreciation, yet it's a good place to start. When someone *really* appreciates something you've done, think about the good feeling it gives you. As I watched myself experience this, I thought, well, if appreciation feels that good when it comes your way, it sure must be worth the time it takes to do it. The joy you receive by appreciating is tremendously increased as you practice it with *deeper levels of sincerity.* Now my "pleases" and "thank you's" have matured into deeper levels of meaning and create a much richer experience in my heart.

It's easy to appreciate people, situations or a new day when things are going great. Here's a first-hand example from a friend who had a lot of good things happen to her all in one day. She says:

"I got accepted to the college of my first choice, my boyfriend gave me roses and my dad told me how proud he was of how well I was doing in school. It was very easy to appreciate that day. I felt great!"

Someone could ask, "But what about the days that seem to go every way except the way we want them to go?" Those are the days when life is a drag, when we feel bored with everything and feel as though we'll never grow up and be out on our own. How can someone appreciate a day like that? Here's an example of one of those draggy days, from the viewpoint of a teenage girl I know. She says:

"I got up one morning, feeling groggy and sluggish. It was rainy and gray outside. I thought to myself that maybe if I dressed up a little it might make me feel better. So I put on one of my favorite outfits. As I was walking toward the front door I ran into my mom, who was on her way to her morning cup of coffee. She took one look at me and said, 'Young lady, there is no way you are going out in the rain dressed like that.' I said, 'But Mom — you don't understand!' That was the beginning of a loud argument that ended up with me changing my clothes and heading off to school with a scowl on my face. I arrived at school and proceeded to get in an argument with my boyfriend about him flirting with one of my girlfriends, and that was just the beginning. What a day this was shaping up to be. All day, my head kept blaming my mom and my boyfriend and trying to figure out what had happened that morning. I needed some help. I felt terrible."

On a day like that I'd use a *super power tool* to pull me back into my heart and help me get the real perspective, so I could at least try to take the bumps in life in stride and hang in for the ride. Appreciation can be that heart power tool to turn an upsetting day into a smooth day. So you might be wondering, "How can I appreciate anything, when it feels like life is just doing me in?" *Appreciating what you do have is a key to help you make life what you want it to be.* You can start by appreciating that things could be worse.

When I start appreciating, I look at it like business. I start by appreciating life itself. After all, life is really a gift. It might not always seem like that's true, but it is. If nothing else, it's a gift of discovery. So I appreciate that!

The girl in the example, through using heart power, finally created thoughts of appreciation that made her feel better. She said to herself, "I appreciate that I even *have* a boyfriend and that even if he's giving me a hard time, deep inside I know he loves me. And, yeah, sometimes it can be frustrating when my mom's telling me what to do; but she really is just trying to take care of me and means no wrong, and I appreciate that." Switching to appreciation, she told me later, really did lift her out of the blues.

Even though it's easier sometimes to let feelings become gloomy, thinking how bad everything is, I always try to snap back and start appreciating. After all, each day is a new beginning, and if each *day* can be a chance to start all over, why couldn't each *moment* be that kind of opportunity?

To really appreciate anything, don't unjustly expect from it. Expecting sets you up for disappointments. Your head might say, "I didn't get what I wanted or deserved." Just try to simply appreciate a situation for not being as bad as it could be. It could be *way* worse. Tough situations are hard to deal with in life because sometimes there is no logical answer as to why. Trying to figure out "whys" causes pain and frustration if you try to understand from the head.I find I do get true understanding if I go to the heart. Trying to figure things out from just the head brings stress to the people I see around me and on TV, so why follow in footsteps that are knee-deep in trouble? Speaking of knees, that reminds me of an example from another friend. Here's what he told me:

"One time I got in a car accident that was not my fault and I broke my knee. No dancing, dating, driving, you name it — no more normal anything for a while! Doesn't sound like much fun, huh? How to appreciate a broken knee, that's a good one, right? Make it simple! I appreciated that it wasn't worse. It could have been my back or my whole life. Appreciating that put me back in my heart. I began to understand the reasons for the broken knee and the gifts that came from it. The main one was a chance to experience and appreciate the care that those who loved me showed, like my mom and dad, friends, etc. It also gave me a chance to slow myself down, giving me a wider view of life, kind of like slowing down long enough to see the flowers on the side of the road. So in the end, even though it could have seemed like a tragedy to have a broken knee, through appreciating, I got a heart understanding of the good that came from it."

So what if we could try to find the good in things *all the time*? Sure, here and there we're big on appreciating everything, on days like Christmas, or Thanksgiving, or Valentine's Day, but what about all those days in between? These special holidays bring a sparkle to people's hearts and bring warm, appreciative feelings because people are making an effort to appreciate their family or friends and remember how lucky they are to have each other.

Well, why not make any day or *every* day a holiday? That's the kind of sparkle and quality that appreciation can bring you. Believe it or not, this is a great game to play with yourself, to bring you more power to control those "off" days.

How does appreciation help you to have this kind of inner control? It gets you in touch with your heart fast, so you can truly be more responsible for your thoughts and feelings throughout the day. When you find your head mulling over a thought that, in turn, creates stress-producing feelings (and hormones), take a mental break and send appreciation to someone you love. It works fast to take you back to your heart computer and helps you in finding a more clear perspective (viewpoint). Appreciate anything — even if it seems silly. Look around you for something to appreciate. Look at a lamp and appreciate Thomas Edison. Look at the carpet and be glad it's not cement. Look at a chair and be happy you don't have to sit on the floor all the time. Appreciate yourself for trying to appreciate. I learned that *anything* can be appreciated. Sometimes, appreciating small things actually makes me laugh to myself at a time when I thought it wasn't possible.

Experiment for awhile and see if appreciation can't add to the sparkle in your life and get those good-feeling hormones going as it did for me. Remember, it takes time to stop and practice because the natural tendency is to be preoccupied with things you want, not the things you give. In my experience, you can get more of what you actually really want by sincerely giving that that you have. Appreciation is a neat place to start. So use your heart smarts to fulfill your want list. I'm outta here.

Earth
One Big Yard, One Body of People

How many people want to contribute to saving the planet? Nowadays a lot of people participate in movements and aggressively defend one side or another of an issue. There are all kinds of pet projects and issues, such as:

- save the whales
- animal rights
- pro-abortion
- anti-abortion
- anti-alcohol/anti-drug
- anti-nuclear campaign
- peace protesters
- pro-America
- Etc., etc.

All of these causes, even the ones against each other, have validity from their point of view and can be fun, but each one only focuses on isolated issues. After all, there are hundreds of these campaigns. Often the anger and stress created by the participants is much more harmful to society than the issues they are trying to change.

So you might ask, "How can I really make a difference to the overall planetary peace and have less confusion?" That's a great question. Well, if we really do care about our planet Earth, we first would need to go to our heart computer and send out care for the planet. We'd start at home and clean up our own backyard. That means starting with yourself. Eliminating your own problems day-to-day, by being in the heart and just loving the people around you, could probably help out more than you realize. If you put efforts into cleaning up your own *stress mess* (cleaning up your own backyard), it creates a very powerful and positive energy that goes out across

Cleaning up the "stress mess" in your own backyard makes a cleaner environment for everyone to live in. Maybe we should start a campaign to save the inner environment.

the planet and actually helps everyone. Have you noticed that when you're feeling up and happy, people around you feel that radiance and often beam it back at you? That's heart radiance!

Here's an example: when I heard about the war starting in the Persian Gulf, I could have become anxious about how the war would affect everybody and worried about everything. I'd been practicing being in the heart for a long time, so I realized that the one thing I could do to help the whole situation was to make sure my own energies stayed deep in my heart, and to love everyone. I appreciated the soldiers and all the leaders involved in the war, even though I wished there were another way to solve the world's differences. This act of appreciation helped me to stay focused in my heart and didn't drag me down. I loved all my friends as much as I could because I realized how precious life is. I noticed that my heart radiance made a difference whenever I met someone who felt unhappy about the war. Now that the war is over, the world is actually more united in a connecting and compassionate way, though quite a way from being united in peace. It makes me appreciate our freedom even more, especially since the war ended so quickly with fewer lives lost than were expected. Heart smarts helped me realize that my friends and neighbors are the most important things in my world, but I've also realized that my world is really everybody's world. We're all in it together; it's ours and the most efficient thing I can do is to practice radiating love and care to all people.

"So what about the help-the-world movements?" you might ask. Don't get me wrong. If you really want to be involved in a movement or a save-the-world campaign, etc., *go for it!* But do yourself and the planet a favor by spending equal time practicing being in the heart and managing your own self. If you want to try a game with it, go ahead and give yourself a week of practicing being in the heart along with campaigning for your favorite *save-the-world* movement. The results might surprise and delight you. Not only would you be helping the mental and emotional conditions around you through heart radiance, but you would be helping the planet as well. And you might even get a new insight (idea), some heart intelligence that would tell you how you could help even more. This could be a good *game plan* for a lifetime of fun and fulfillment. After all, we're all on planet Earth together.

Looking down from above, the planet is just one big yard with one body of people. They are all connected in the heart yet they are not heart smart enough to realize that at this time. As individuals learn to connect more with their own heart, this will activate the hope for a family-style global communication and basic peace in the future. If today's teenagers become heart smart, then the planet stands a chance to negotiate future peace with love and not war. So as you grow up and want to campaign for an issue, you may want to invest in promoting self-peace through self-management, by learning to follow heart, not head, directives. I know that was a long sentence, but the planet has been waiting a long time for that to happen. Let's make it happen.

Here's a fun game: unscramble the word "earth." You may discover what could be the true evolution of planet Earth:

PLANET

18

Let's Wrap it Up
Heart Smarts Practices

The following handy "Ready Reference Pages" of typical teenage situations can help bail you out quickly, *if* you practice using your *heart smarts*. Use them whenever you are in your head and can't quite access your creative heart program, or when you need a practical example of a creative heart program to do. These pages can be helpful — right when you most need them. They can save you a lot of stressful wear and tear. Most of the time when you're not in your heart, you'll probably find one of the situations described that comes close to applying to you. Sure, there are extreme situations where it doesn't seem like anything can help. But practice on smaller situations, then the more serious problems can be dealt with as you learn to access the power of your heart. There are always exceptions, and I will be covering more examples and situations in future writings.

A Few Heart Smarts Practices
(Ready Reference Pages)

Situation: **A friend (or friends) snubs you.**

Head Reaction:

Resentment! Judge them or try to expose their faults. Get mad and not talk to them. Talk behind their backs.

A Heart Smart Response:

Love yourself and realize you're okay anyhow. Go to your heart for your real security. You can't depend on their approval to feel good about yourself. Security has to come from within you. Send them love and neutralize the negative energy. Besides, your friend could have been out of her heart and having a bad day.

Situation: **You're afraid you won't get that date you want so much.**

Head Reaction:

You become anxious, insecure and preoccupied with that one desire and stress starts to multiply.

A Heart Smart Response:

Realize your world really won't blow up whichever way the date goes. Find a deep *heart* attitude and chill out so your *head* won't drive you crazy with overcare. Strong fears and anxieties especially drain your system. Stay centered in the heart so relationships can add to you but not take away from you if they don't turn out to suit you.

<u>Situation</u>: You have a teacher you don't like and just can't communicate with.

Head Reaction:

You feel misunderstood and make negative remarks to other people behind the teacher's back. You harbor constant resentments towards the teacher.

A Heart Smart Response:

Go deeper in your heart and project yourself into the teacher's situation. Realize the pressure a teacher can be under dealing with that many people at a time. Make efforts to send love energy from your heart to the teacher, instead of resentment. Many times this works wonders to establish a better communication. It's tricky to remember to send love rather than resentment when you feel you have a legal gripe. *Practice learning that trick.* It's worth it.

<u>Situation</u>: You feel a parent (or parents) just doesn't understand you.

Head Reaction:

Withdraw from them. Stop communicating. Do things to upset them for attention. Lie or rebel.

A Heart Smart Response:

Teenagers and parents sometimes sit down to have what they call a heart-to-heart talk. As disagreements arise, it becomes a head-to-head talk and ends up in a "scream fest" with no solution. Instead, try it this way: send love to them before you talk and ask them if they'd play the game of deep heart listening with you. Remind each other to go back to the heart if the energy starts getting into head reactions, which cause friction. By trying to listen to and understand parents from deeper levels, it can cause their respect for you to increase, resulting in deeper communication as time goes on. Don't just try this once and blow up; remember, all of this takes practice.

Situation: **A friend dropped out of school (or got pregnant, got in an accident, had to move away, isn't allowed to see you anymore, etc., etc.)**

Head Reaction:

You over-worry, become emotionally drained from a sense of loss, start to have less fun with other friends and family, etc.

A Heart Smart Response:

It's Heart Smart to have care and compassion for a friend with a problem. The *heart* puts out compassion that can comfort and help. The *head* causes you to overcare and get over-involved in people's problems resulting in both parties getting drained. *You can't help people if you allow yourself to be dragged down and drained by their lumps and bumps in life.* You *can* help by loving them from the heart and learning the difference between true care and over-involvement. By being responsible for yourself you can really help them more and maintain balance in your own system at the same time. That's Self-Discovery.

<u>Situation:</u> You feel you don't fit in.

Head Reaction:

I'm not cool. Something must be wrong with me. I don't have talents. I'm not as smart as they are, etc.

A Heart Smart Response:

As you practice connecting with your own heart, you realize more and more that the security you're looking for from your friends is within you. As you realize this at deeper levels your self-esteem increases. You magically start to fit in more places than you would expect. The confidence you build, by listening to and following your heart, keeps you from overcaring whether you fit into certain situations or not. As you develop confidence in yourself you will magnetize more friends to you, because people tend to be drawn to a person who is building their self-esteem. Take about *five* minutes a day and focus in your heart. Send out love and caring feelings towards someone or appreciation towards someone who has helped you, or just appreciate the gift of life. *Since heart frequencies balance your system, you will find self-esteem developing in many areas of your life just by the practice of radiating love.* It may not seem like that would have anything to do with building self-esteem, yet it could be the quickest way to self-esteem. Perhaps it has just been overlooked because it's so simple. This is a serious Heart Smarts tip. Discover for yourself but remember, **practice**.

Situation: I'm bored with life or I don't feel like it (whether homework, chores, coming home on time, being kind to sisters and brothers, etc., or even practicing Heart Smarts).

Head Reaction:

Sulk, mope around, look for stimulation in the wrong places. Feel frustrated. Rebel and resist. Try to find ways to get out of doing something. Make up excuses.

A Heart Smart Response:

Boredom is temporary saturation with the things you usually chase for stimulation. The way to beat boredom is to find the balance in what you do to stimulate your life. If you're into TV watching, partying, sports, hobbies, or other types of stimulation, you need a balance of the following: the practice of managing your mental and emotional energies; the practice of taking on certain responsibilities in your physical world — taking care of your body and certain household responsibilities and school. This gives you well-roundedness and deeper inner respect and, therefore, much more self-esteem. If you practice listening to and following your heart a few minutes a day, you'll develop a balanced decision-making process. Constant party-type fun stimulates the mind, but learning bottom-line responsibility can be fun also, because it helps your whole system feel better and more complete. So the Heart Smarts equation would be to mix your fun event-type stimulation with equal proportion of balanced responsibility. This equals out to peace and more true *continuous* excitement in life. Boredom accumulates stress — a *stress buster* disintegrates boredom. Play with following your heart directives for awhile and learn to meet the real you.

To sum it up, you have more power to zap the misery out of your life than you would even start to believe. So don't condemn me as wrong until you sincerely practice heart listening and heart action which leads to Heart Smarts. Then away with boredom and in with fun. Self-management leads to some of the highest fun you could have. I probably over-talked this time, but I'm through. Go have a good talk with yourself and go for it. Let's rock!

So here you are at the beginning of your next moment. Just remember what your heart can do. As you practice accessing heart power, it will show you that your heart computer really is your best buddy. *The more you discover the difference between your head thoughts and your heart directives, the smarter you'll become, leading to the mastery of true fun.* As you get good at using the tools in this book, you're well on your way to building your own personal problem-solving computer. What a fun convenience that would be! Trust me, *it* will work if you work *it*.

A few reminders: keep communication open within yourself and with the people in your life. Remember —*communicate as you go, don't wait 'til you blow* — to help others understand you better. Cut yourself slack (forgive and understand, have patience with yourself) as you change and grow, but don't forget to practice. As you start to change yourself, that helps to create changes in the people around you. However, don't worry about whether others change or not. Just dig in your heart and find your own peace. That's your first responsibility — self-management. The real fun starts as you come into your own security — the true self-esteem that you're looking for! Remember, being a **stress buster** is your gift to yourself and others. Unwrap that gift, discover your real self, and let's *"wage war on stress"* together.

Let's rock,

The Doc

❖THE INSTITUTE OF HEARTMATH

The Institute of HeartMath is a non-profit educational and research organization founded by Doc Lew Childre. The Institute has developed a system of energy-efficiency and self-empowerment called HeartMath™ to help people develop greater self-management, self-esteem, and reduce stress.

The Institute offers seminars based on the HeartMath system for businesses, schools, non-profit agencies, groups, the military, and families. Seminars are presented in a variety of formats, including school in-services, in-house staff development, as well as customized "learning vacations," including whitewater rafting trips, dude ranches, ski trips, and other fun experiences.

The HEART SMARTS seminars are designed for educators, parents, and young people, and are based on the principles outlined in this book. EMPOWERING THE GIFTED CHILD is designed for gifted and talented students, parents and educators.

The EMPOWERING THE HEART OF BUSINESS seminar is designed to help businesses increase care and efficiency based on the techniques outlined in the book, *Self Empowerment: The Heart Approach to Stress Management; Common Sense Strategies*, by Doc Lew Childre.

The HEART EMPOWERMENT seminars are for individuals and non-profit organizations seeking creative ways to empower their personal mission while reducing stress. RECOVERY TO DISCOVERY seminars are designed for people in recovery from addictive behaviors, as well as substance abuse professionals. Both of these seminars are based on the book, *The Hidden Power of the Heart*, by Sara Paddison.

For more information on seminars, contact:
THE INSTITUTE OF HEARTMATH
P.O. Box 1463 • Boulder Creek, CA 95006
408-338-6803 • 800-354-6284 • Fax 408-338-9861

HEART ZONES:
A Musical Solution for Stress
by Doc Lew Childre

"Music is like a food for the psyche. Unbalanced food leads to negative feedback in your system, whether it be physical food or food for the psyche (music, impressions, color, thoughts, etc.)," according to Doc Lew Childre, composer of *Heart Zones*. Both young people and adults benefit from the right "vitamin-charged food."

"The Doc" designed *Heart Zones* to facilitate stress release and create an enhanced learning environment, while adding fun and balance to your mental and emotional well-being.

> "I enjoyed **Heart Zones**. Very beneficial for stress management."
> **David J. Fletcher, M.D., Occupational and Preventive Medicine, Midwest Occupational Health Associates**

"**Heart Zones** is excellent for deep muscular relaxation. As a therapeutic tape, it is very different from all similar products I have used before. The compositions are inspirational and a refreshing change from the albums sold as 'New Age'. It's a whole new genre of music."
Marshall Gilula, M.D., Psychiatrist

"It really really works. When I need to relax, I put on cut four. When I need to get going in the morning with a positive attitude, it's cut one. When it's time to write or get something done in a hurry, cut three brings focus and speed. The effects are discreet and effective and the instrumentation and presentation are right on the mark. [Heart Zones] is responsible for my high productivity!"
Scott Schuster, Editorial Director, Executive Programs, national magazine

Cassette $9.95 • Compact disc $15.98 plus shipping and handling

SELF EMPOWERMENT:
The Heart Approach to Stress Management; Common Sense Strategies
by Doc Lew Childre

In this practical and timely book, Doc Lew Childre offers effective common sense strategies that can empower you to relieve the stress of today's personal, family, social and business problems. Topics include:

- Intui-technology™—the science of intuitive development
- The advantages of the men's and women's movements
- Intuitive levels of time management
- How to balance your inner female/male nature
- Techniques to eliminate relationship drains
- How to care without stress from overcare
- The family concept—the business trend for efficiency and effectiveness
- Sexual harassment—the intelligence beyond it
- Strategies for finally being your true self
- Accessing the power of your "heart intuition"

"The message is a strong one and the methodology can be understood and adopted by many. The potential release of positive energy is formidable."
J. Tracy O'Rourke, Chairman and CEO, Varian Associates

"Now here's the book for people who are really serious about improving their lives. A refreshingly hopeful and positive vision of the world [that] can transform the workplace, the schoolroom, the home, and all social situations."
Dr. Joyce Chumbley, Educational consultant

$13.95 (paper); $22.95 (cloth) plus shipping and handling

THE HIDDEN POWER OF THE HEART:
Achieving Balance and Fulfillment
in a Stressful World
by Sara Paddison

In this wonderful book, you will learn that each one of us has a magnificent power within us that can facilitate change, eliminate stress and empower us to live to our fullest potential. The secret for uncovering this power is learning to live life from the heart. You will discover:

- How to eliminate fear, anxiety and insecurity through heart understanding.
- How to use the natural intelligence of the heart to make life work in more efficient ways.
- How to increase your capacity for stress reduction.
- How to build a strong foundation for self-security that facilitates adapting to change.
- How to take charge of your life through mental and emotional management—the key to self empowerment.
- How to create a nourishing family atmosphere at home and work.
- How to put simplicity back into life for more quality returns.
- How to deepen relationships with your family, partner, friends and co-workers.

The Hidden Power of the Heart describes the knowingness and power available to everyone within themselves. This book explains how to access the individual power within each one of us and apply it practically in daily life.

$11.95 plus shipping and handling • Available Fall '92

Ordering Information

To order books, tapes, and compact discs, please send
check, money order or credit card information to:

Planetary Publications
P.O. Box 66 • 14700 West Park Ave.
Boulder Creek, California, 95006
408-338-2161/ 800-372-3100 • Fax 408-338-9861

- Please include shipping and handling costs: $2.50
  for first item, $1.00 each additional item (book rate).
- For UPS delivery, add $1.00 to total shipping and
  handling. (Foreign residents should double the
  shipping and handling rates.)
- California residents include 7.25% sales tax.
- Visa, Mastercard, and American Express accepted.
  Please include expiration date, card number and
  full name on card.
- For convenience, place your order using our toll-
  free number — 800-372-3100, 24 hours a day, 7
  days a week, or fax us your order at 408-338-9861.